Poems and Readings for
# Christenings and
# Naming Ceremonies

# Poems and Readings for
# Christenings and
# Naming Ceremonies

Compiled by

## Susannah Steel

NEW
HOLLAND

Published in 2009 by New Holland Publishers (UK) Ltd
London • Cape Town • Sydney • Auckland
www.newhollandpublishers.com
Garfield House, 86–88 Edgware Road, London W2 2EA, United Kingdom
80 McKenzie Street, Cape Town 8001, South Africa
Unit 1, 66 Gibbes Street, Chatswood, NSW 2067, Australia
218 Lake Road, Northcote, Auckland, New Zealand

10 9 8 7 6 5 4 3 2 1

Text copyright © 2009 Susannah Steel
Copyright © 2009 New Holland Publishers (UK) Ltd
Susannah Steel has asserted her moral right to be identified as the author of
this work.
*Copyright acknowledgements can be found on pages 186–188*

A catalogue record for this book is available from the British Library

ISBN 978 1 84773 403 7

Publishing Director: Rosemary Wilkinson
Publisher: Aruna Vasudevan
Project Editor: Julia Shone
Editorial Assistant: Cosima Hibbert
Design: Sarah Williams
DTP: Pete Gwyer
Production: Melanie Dowland

Reproduction by Pica Digital Pte. Ltd., Singapore
Printed and bound in India by Replika Press

The paper used to produce this book is sourced from sustainable forests.

*To Rosie,*
*who is a great blessing.*

# Contents

# Foreword

Welcoming a new baby into the world can be one of the most joyous events we experience in life, but for many of us the excitement of parenthood may be mixed with a feeling of trepidation. All our love, hopes, dreams and fears are focused on a tiny baby and an unknown future. For parents alone to give their children everything they need to cope with life – a sense of identity, love, joy, motivation, friendship, strength, contentment, knowledge and wisdom – can seem a daunting challenge. So a Christening or a Naming Ceremony is a natural rite of passage in which we can give thanks for a child's life, ask for a blessing on them, formally name them and make promises, with the support of family and friends, to ensure his or her future welfare and happiness.

This selection of poems and readings is an attempt to explore some of the emotions, promises and duties that accompany this moment of affirmation: of powerful, unconditional love; the delight of the young and the freedom of youth; expectations and hopes for the future; spiritual blessings and guidance; and the roles and responsibilities that fall on parents and godparents, or 'guide parents', to support, instruct and encourage a child throughout life. If you are an adult being baptized, I hope you find a reading that echoes your sentiments about wanting to live a new life.

However you mark this unique celebration, I hope that it is a wonderfully happy and memorable beginning.

–Susannah Steel

# Advice on Different Services

One of the first things you need to decide is the kind of service
you would like to have. There are several options available
depending on how religious or non-religious you are, including:

## Christenings

In the Christian church, a Christening, or Baptism, is known as
a sacrament – a ceremony that is a visible sign of faith in God
and Jesus Christ, and of God's love. It is a public act of asking
for God's blessing on the birth of a child – or, in the case of a
baptism, the spiritual 'rebirth' of an adult – and their future
life. It also marks the start of a journey of faith.

Christenings are usually part of a Sunday service. They involve
parents and godparents making a series of declarations on behalf
of the child, and agreeing to pray for and support them. Any
readings are usually read out at the end of the ceremony after the
minister has sprinkled water, which symbolizes purification, over
the child, made a sign of the cross on their forehead and lit a
candle to symbolize his or her life being a light shining in the
world. Talk to your minister beforehand about which reading or
poem you want to use; depending on your minister, there should
be plenty of scope to choose what appeals to you personally.

## Thanksgiving Services

You may prefer to have a Thanksgiving service in a church, where
you thank God for the gift of your baby and your baby is blessed,
but you don't make the same declaration of faith and promises
as in a Christening service. Again, you will need to check with
your minister first about which reading or poem you might like
to include after the blessing.

**Naming Ceremonies**

Civil Naming Ceremonies and humanist Baby Namings are
alternatives to a religious service. Civil Naming Ceremonies are
offered by most United Kingdom local authorities through their
register offices: the ceremony is performed by a professional
celebrant in an approved venue and includes an introduction
and welcome, a reading, the naming of the child and the
promises of the parents and supporting adults. No religious
readings are allowed at these ceremonies, but you can include
other additional readings if you wish.

Humanist Baby Namings can be held at home, at a special venue,
or as a formal welcome at the start of a celebratory party. A
humanist celebrant, or someone whom the parents have chosen,
leads the ceremony: the baby is formally named and the parents
declare their love for their child and give promises, as do those
relatives or friends who have been asked to be mentors. Any non-
religious poems and readings are allowed at these ceremonies.

# How to Use This Book

Organised alphabetically by author surname, *Poems and Readings
for Christenings and Naming Ceremonies* includes traditional and
contemporary, biblical and non-religious readings from a wide
range of sources. Each entry has a helpful tag in the top margin
of the page indicating what the extract is and a short biography
about the author. The book ends with a selection of humorous
quotations and an index of first lines for those who only know the
first line of a reading or a poem but do not know the actual title.

With these useful guides, we hope you will find a suitable piece to
read at the Christening or Naming ceremony of a loved one.

# Song from Lily-Bell and Thistledown

POEM

LOUISA MAY ALCOTT

Awake! Awake! for the earliest gleam
Of golden sunlight shines
On the rippling waves, that brightly flow
Beneath the flowering vines.
Awake! Awake! for the low, sweet chant
Of the wild-birds' morning hymn
Comes floating by on the fragrant air,
Through the forest cool and dim;
Then spread each wing,
And work, and sing,
Through the long, bright sunny hours;
O'er the pleasant earth
We journey forth,
For a day among the flowers.
Awake! Awake! for the summer wind
Hath bidden the blossoms unclose,
Hath opened the violet's soft blue eye,
And awakened the sleeping rose.
And lightly they wave on their slender stems
Fragrant, and fresh, and fair,
Waiting for us, as we singing come
To gather our honey-dew there.
Then spread each wing,
And work, and sing,
Through the long, bright sunny hours;
O'er the pleasant earth
We journey forth,
For a day among the flowers.

15

*Louisa May Alcott (1832–1888) is one of America's best-loved authors
and is most famous for her children's book,* Little Women, *and its sequels. She
also wrote poems and other moralistic stories for children. This poem appears
in a short story from the collection* Flower Fairies.

POEM

# A Baby Will Make Love Stronger

ANON

A baby will make love stronger
Days shorter, Nights longer
Bankroll smaller, Clothes shabbier,
The past forgotten,
And the future worth living for.

POEM

# A Christening Prayer

ANON

A special prayer for your baby
and all the family too;
May God grant many blessings
on this special day for you.
May He bless you with joy and happiness
and show you every day,
His love is there to guide you
every step along life's way.

# A Poem for Parents

POEM

ANON

There are little eyes upon you,
And they are watching night and day;
There are little ears that quickly
Take in every word you say.

There are little hands all eager
To do everything you do;
and a little boy who's dreaming
Of the day he'll be like you.

You're the little fellow's idol;
You're the wisest of the wise;
In his little mind, about you
No suspicions ever rise.

He believes in you devotedly,
Holds that all you say and do,
He will say and do in your way
When he's grown up like you.

There's a wide-eyed little fellow
Who believes you're always right;
And his ears are always open,
And he watches day and night.

You are setting an example
Every day in all you do;
For the little boy who's waiting
To grow up to be just like you.

PRAYER

# A Prayer Celebrating the Spirit of a Child

ANON

Give us the spirit of the child.

Give us the child who lives within –
the child who trusts,
the child who imagines,
the child who sings,
the child who receives without reservation,
the child who gives without judgement.

Give us a child's eyes,
that we may receive the beauty
and freshness of this day like a sunrise.
Give us a child's ears,
that we may hear
the music of mythical times.

Give us a child's heart,
that we may be filled with wonder and delight.

Give us a child's faith,
that we may be cured of our cynicism.

Give us the spirit of the child,
who is not afraid to need,
who is not afraid to love.

Amen

# All We Need Is the Truth in Our Hand
ANON

All we need is the truth in our hand.
Someone to call a friend.
Never fear the darkness.
All we need is just the sun in the sky.
And the hope of a summer to come with the meaning of love.

# Be True to Those Who Trust Thee
ANON

Be true to those who trust thee,
Be pure for those who care.
Be strong, for there is much to suffer,
Be brave, for there is much to dare.

Be a friend to all – the foe, the friendless.
Be giving and forget the gift.
Be humble, for thou knowest thy weakness.
And then, look up and laugh and love and live.

## Celtic Blessing (1)

ANON

May the strength of the wind and the light of the sun,
The softness of the rain and the mystery of the moon
Reach you and fill you.
May beauty delight you and happiness uplift you,
May wonder fulfil you and love surround you.
May your step be steady and your arm be strong,
May your heart be peaceful and your word be true.
May you seek to learn, may you learn to live,
May you live to love, and may you love – always.

## Celtic Blessing (2)

ANON

God be with you in every pass,
Jesus be with you on every hill,
Spirit be with you on every stream,
Headland and ridge and lawn;
Each sea and land, each moor and meadow,
Each lying down, each rising up,
In the trough of the waves, on the crest of the billows,
Each step of the journey you go.

# Hong Kong Proverb

ANON

POEM

As long as we have hope,
we have direction,
the energy to move,
and the map to move by.

We have a hundred alternatives,
a thousand paths and infinity of dreams.
Hopeful, we are halfway to where we want to go;
Hopeless, we are lost forever.

21

# Hush, Little Baby

ANON

Hush, little baby, don't say a word,
Mama's going to buy you a mockingbird.

If that mockingbird won't sing,
Mama's going to buy you a diamond ring.

If that diamond ring turns brass,
Mama's going to buy you a looking glass.

If that looking glass gets broke,
Mama's going to buy you a billy goat.

If that billy goat won't pull,
Mama's going to buy you a cart and bull.

If that cart and bull turn over,
Mama's going to buy you a dog named Rover.

If that dog named Rover won't bark,
Mama's going to buy you a horse and cart.

If that horse and cart fall down,
You'll still be the sweetest little boy in town.

So hush little baby, don't you cry,
Daddy loves you and so do I.

# Iona* Community Prayer

ANON

Deep peace of the running wave to you
Deep peace of the flowing air to you
Deep peace of the quiet earth to you
Deep peace of the shining stars to you
Deep peace of the Son of Peace to you

*The Iona Community is a Christian community whose aims include
peace and social justice, rebuilding of community and the renewal of worship.
Members meet regularly throughout the year in local groups
and in four plenary gatherings, including a week on Iona.

23

# May Beauty Delight You

ANON

May beauty delight you and happiness uplift you,
May wonder fulfil you and love surround you.
May your step be steady and your arm be strong,
May your heart be peaceful and your word be true.
May you seek to learn, may you learn to live,
May you live to love, and may you love – always.

If children live with security, they learn to have faith;
If children live with approval, they learn to
   like themselves;
If children live with love around them, they learn to
   give love to the world.

BLESSING # Navajo* Blessing for a Newborn Child

ANON

Today we are blessed with a beautiful baby.

May his feet be to the east.
May his right hand be to the south.
May his head be to the west.
May his left hand be to the north.

May he walk and dwell on Mother Earth peacefully.
May he be blessed with precious, variegated stones.
May he be blessed with fat sheep in variation.
May he be blessed with respectful relatives and friends.
May he be blessed with the essence of life in old age.
May he be blessed with the source of happiness in beauty.
We ask all these blessings with reverence and holiness.

My Mother the Earth.
My Father the Sky.
My Sister the Sun.

All is Peace.
All is Beauty.
All is Happiness.
All is Harmony.

*The Navajo Tribe is recognised as the largest Native American tribe
in the United States. According to the 2000 census there are 298,215
Navajo people living throughout the United States.

# Omaha* Native American Blessing

ANON

BLESSING

Sun, Moon, Stars, all you that move in the heavens, hear us!
Into your midst has come a new life.
Make his/her path smooth, that he/she may reach the brow
of the first hill!

Winds, Clouds, Rain, Mist, all you that move in the air, hear us!
Into your midst has come a new life.
Make his/her path smooth, that he/she may reach the brow
of the second hill!

Hills, Valleys, Rivers, Lakes, Trees, Grasses, all you of the
earth, hear us!
Into your midst has come a new life.
Make his/her path smooth, that he/she may reach the brow
of the third hill!

Birds, great and small, that fly in the air,
Animals, great and small, that dwell in the forest,
Insects that creep among the grasses and burrow in the
ground, hear us!
Into your midst has come a new life.
Make his/her path smooth, that he/she may reach the brow
of the fourth hill!

All you of the heavens, all you of the air, all you of the
earth, hear us!
Into your midst has come a new life.
Make his/her path smooth, then shall he/she travel beyond
the four hills!

*The language of the Omaha Native Americans belongs to the
Siouan branch of the Hokan-Siouan linguistic stock. They
traditionally live along the Missouri River in Ohio and Nebraska.

# Prayer of the Orthodox Church

ANON

O Lord our God,
look mercifully on us
and on those who are preparing
for Holy Baptism
and have their heads bowed before you now:
make the light of your Gospel
shine upon them;
send an angel of light
to deliver them from all powers of the enemy,
that when they are fit to receive your immortal gift
and are brought into a life
of obedience to your commandments,
they may know the joys of heaven.
For you are their light
and we glorify you,
Father, Son and Holy Spirit,
now and for ever
to the ages of ages.

Amen

# Precious One

ANON

Precious one, so small, so sweet,
Dancing in on angel feet
Straight from Heaven's brightest star
What a miracle you are!

# Risk

ANON

To laugh is to risk appearing a fool.
To weep is to risk appearing sentimental.
To reach out to another is to risk involvement.
To expose your feelings is to risk rejection.
To place your dreams before the crowd is to risk ridicule.
To love is to risk not being loved in return.
To go forward in the face of overwhelming odds
is to risk failure.
But risks must be taken,
because the greatest risk of all is to risk nothing.
The person who risks nothing, does nothing,
has nothing and is nothing.
He may avoid suffering and sorrow,
but he cannot learn, he cannot feel,
he cannot change, he cannot grow
and he cannot love.
Chained by his certitudes, he is a slave.
Only the person who risks is truly free.

BLESSING

# Traditional Irish Blessing (1)

ANON

May the road rise to meet you,
May the wind be always at your back.
May the sun shine warm upon your face,
The rains fall soft upon your fields.
And until we meet again,
May God hold you in the palm of his hand.

May God be with you and bless you;
May you see your children's children.
May you be poor in misfortune,
Rich in blessings,
May you know nothing but happiness
From this day forward.

May the road rise to meet you
May the wind be always at your back
May the warm rays of sun fall upon your home
And may the hand of a friend always be near.
May green be the grass you walk on,
May blue be the skies above you,
May pure be the joys that surround you,
May true be the hearts that love you.

# Traditional Irish Blessing (2)

ANON

BLESSING

May you always have walls for the winds,
A roof for the rain, tea beside the fire,
Laughter to cheer you, those you love near you,
and all your heart might desire.

May the sun shine all day long,
Everything go right, and nothing wrong.
May those you love bring love back to you,
And may all the wishes you wish come true.

May luck be your friend
In whatever you do
And may trouble be always
A stranger to you.

BLESSING

# Traditional Scottish Blessing

ANON

May there always be work for your hands to do.
May your purse always hold a coin or two.
May the sun always shine upon your window pane.
May a rainbow be certain to follow each rain.
May the hand of a friend always be near to you and
May God fill your heart with gladness to cheer you.

PRAYER

# Traditional Zuni* Indian Prayer

ANON

Now this is the day.
Our child,
Into the daylight
You will go standing.
Preparing for your day.

Our child, it is your day,
This day.

May your road be fulfilled.
In your thoughts may we live,
May we be the ones whom your thoughts will embrace,
May you help us all to finish our roads.

*The Zuni Native American tribe has a population of 7,758, living
on the Zuni Indian Reservation in New Mexico, surrounded by the
Zuni Mountains and the Cibola National Forest. The Zuni Tribe is
governed by an elected governor, lieutenant governor, and a six-member
Tribal Council with elections held every four years.

# What Folks Are Made Of

A N O N

POEM

What are little babies made of, made of?
What are little babies made of?
Diapers and crumbs and sucking their thumbs;
That's what little babies are made of?

What are little boys made of, made of?
What are little boys made of?
Snips and snails and puppy-dog tails;
That's what little boys are made of.

What are little girls made of, made of?
What are little girls made of?
Sugar and spice and everything nice;
That's what little girls are made of ...

31

*The second and third stanzas of this poem are the most famous but
actually form part of the longer piece,* What Folks Are Made Of. *Two
stanzas, including the second one are usually attributed to Robert Southey
(1774–1843), an English poet and historian, who became poet laureate in 1813.*

# Which Day Are You?

ANON

Mondays child is fair of face,
Tuesdays child is full of grace,
Wednesdays child is full of woe,
Thursdays child has far to go,
Fridays child is loving and giving,
Saturdays child works hard for his living,
And the child that is born on the Sabbath day
Is bonny and blithe, and good and gay.

# The Future

MATTHEW ARNOLD

A wanderer is man from his birth.
He was born in a ship
On the breast of the river of Time;
Brimming with wonder and joy
He spreads out his arms to the light,
Rivets his gaze on the banks of the stream.

As what he sees is, so have his thoughts been.
Whether he wakes,
Where the snowy mountainous pass,
Echoing the screams of the eagles,
Hems in its gorges the bed
Of the new-born clear-flowing stream;
Whether he first sees light
Where the river in gleaming rings
Sluggishly winds through the plain;
Whether in sound of the swallowing sea –
As is the world on the banks,
So is the mind of the man.

Vainly does each, as he glides,
Fable and dream
Of the lands which the river of Time
Had left ere he woke on its breast,
Or shall reach when his eyes have been closed.
Only the tract where he sails
He wots of; only the thoughts,
Raised by the objects he passes, are his.

Who can see the green earth any more
As she was by the sources of Time?
Who imagines her fields as they lay
In the sunshine, unworn by the plough?
Who thinks as they thought,
The tribes who then roamed on her breast,
Her vigorous, primitive sons?

What girl
Now reads in her bosom as clear
As Rebekah read, when she sate
At eve by the palm-shaded well?
Who guards in her breast
As deep, as pellucid a spring
Of feeling, as tranquil, as sure?

What bard,
At the height of his vision, can deem
Of God, of the world, of the soul,
With a plainness as near,
As flashing as Moses felt
When he lay in the night by his flock
On the starlit Arabian waste?
Can rise and obey
The beck of the Spirit like him?

This tract which the river of Time
Now flows through with us, is the plain.
Gone is the calm of its earlier shore.
Bordered by cities and hoarse
With a thousand cries is its stream.
And we on its breast, our minds
Are confused as the cries which we hear,
Changing and shot as the sights which we see.

And we say that repose has fled
For ever the course of the river of Time.
That cities will crowd to its edge
In a blacker, incessanter line;
That the din will be more on its banks,
Denser the trade on its stream,
Flatter the plain where it flows,
Fiercer the sun overhead;
That never will those on its breast
See an ennobling sight,
Drink of the feeling of quiet again.

But what was before us we know not,
And we know not what shall succeed.

Haply, the river of Time –
As it grows, as the towns on its marge
Fling their wavering lights
On a wider, statelier stream –
May acquire, if not the calm
Of its early mountainous shore,
Yet a solemn peace of its own.

And the width of the waters, the hush
Of the grey expanse where he floats,
Freshening its current and spotted with foam
As it draws to the Ocean, may strike
Peace to the soul of the man on its breast –
As the pale waste widens around him,
As the banks fade dimmer away,
As the stars come out, and the night-wind
Brings up the stream
Murmurs and scents of the infinite sea.

*Matthew Arnold (1822–1888) was an English poet and critic who also worked as a school inspector. His interest in education and Victorian values influenced his writings, and his transparent poetic style influenced later poets such as W. B. Yeats (*see pages 176–179*) and Sylvia Plath (*see pages 133–134*).*

# You Begin

POEM

MARGARET ATWOOD

You begin this way:
this is your hand,
this is your eye,
this is a fish, blue and flat
on the paper, almost
the shape of an eye
This is your mouth, this is an O
or a moon, whichever
you like. This is yellow.

Outside the window
is the rain, green
because it is summer, and beyond that
the trees and then the world,
which is round and has only
the colours of these nine crayons.

This is the world, which is fuller
and more difficult to learn than I have said.
You are right to smudge it that way
with the red and then
the orange: the world burns.

Once you have learned these words
you will learn that there are more
words than you can ever learn.
The word hand floats above your hand
like a small cloud over a lake.

The word hand anchors
your hand to this table
your hand is a warm stone
I hold between two words.

This is your hand, these are my hands, this is the world,
which is round but not flat and has more colours
than we can see.
It begins, it has an end,
this is what you will
come back to, this is your hand.

*Margaret Atwood* (b. 1939) *is an award-winning Canadian author. She has been writing for over 35 years during which time she has written more than 40 books including novels, short stories, poetry and books for children.*

# from Letter to Frank Austen*

JANE AUSTEN

POEM

My dearest Frank, I wish you joy
Of Mary's safety with a Boy,
Whose birth has given little pain
Compared with that of Mary Jane.
May he a growing Blessing prove,
And well deserve his Parents' Love!
Endow'd with Art's and Nature's Good,
Thy name possessing with thy Blood,
In him, in all his ways, may we
Another Francis William see!–
Thy infant days may he inherit,
Thy warmth, nay insolence of spirit; –
We would not with one fault dispense
To weaken the resemblance.
May he revive thy Nursery sin,
Peeping as daringly within,
(His curley Locks but just descried)
With 'Bet, my be not come to bide.'
Fearless of danger, braving pain,
And threaten'd very oft in vain,
Still may one Terror daunt his soul,
One needful engine of controul
Be found in this sublime array,
A neighbouring Donkey's aweful Bray!
So may his equal faults as Child,
Produce Maturity as mild.

His saucy words and fiery ways
In early Childhood's pettish days,
In Manhood shew his Father's mind,
Like him, considerate and kind;
All Gentleness to those around,
And eager only not to wound.
Then like his Father too, he must,
To his own former struggles just,
Feel his Deserts with honest Glow,
And all his self-improvement know.
A native fault may thus give birth
To the best blessing, conscious worth.

*This is taken from Jane Austen's letter to her brother Frank,
dated 26 July 1809. Austen wrote this in the form of a poem,
congratulating her brother on the birth of his second child, a son.

*Jane Austen (1775–1817) was the daughter of a clergyman, and although
she never married and had children she was part of a close-knit family. She is most
famous for her witty, insightful novels about the English middle and upper classes.*

# Prayer for Kindness

BAHÁ'ULLÁH

Be generous in prosperity, and thankful in adversity.
Be fair in thy judgment, and guarded in thy speech.
Be a lamp unto those who walk in darkness, and a
home to the stranger.
Be eyes to the blind, and a guiding light unto the
feet of the erring.
Be a breath of life to the body of humankind,
a dew to the soil of the human heart, and a fruit
upon the tree of humility.

*Bahá'Ulláh (1817–1892) was the founder of the Baha'I faith, which
believes that all people are equal, they belong to one human family, and that
there is one God for all people.*

POEM

# A Cradle Song
## from Songs of Innocence
WILLIAM BLAKE

Sweet dreams, form a shade,
O'er my lovely infant's head;
Sweet dreams of pleasant streams,
By happy, silent, moony beams.

Sweet sleep, with soft down
Weave thy brows an infant crown.
Sweet sleep, Angel mild,
Hover o'er my happy child.

Sweet smiles, in the night,
Hover over my delight;
Sweet smiles, mother's smiles,
All the livelong night beguiles.

Sweet moans, dovelike sighs,
Chase not slumber from thy eyes.
Sweet moans, sweeter smiles,
All the dovelike moans beguiles.

Sleep, sleep, happy child,
All creation slept and smil'd;
Sleep, sleep, happy sleep,
While o'er thee thy mother weep.

Sweet babe, in thy face
Holy image I can trace.
Sweet babe, once like thee,
Thy maker lay and wept for me,

Wept for me, for thee, for all,
When he was an infant small.
Thou his image ever see,
Heavenly face that smiles on thee,

Smiles on thee, on me, on all;
Who became an infant small.
Infant smiles are his own smiles,
Heaven and earth to peace beguiles.

*William Blake (1757–1827) was an English artist and poet and part of the English Romantic movement.* Songs of Innocence, *written in 1789, was a collection of poems written from a child's point of view.*

POEM

# Eternity

WILLIAM BLAKE

He who binds to himself a joy
Does the wingéd life destroy;
But he who kisses the joy as it flies
Lives in eternity's sun rise.

POEM

# Infant Joy

WILLIAM BLAKE

**44**
_____

'I have no name:
I am but two days old.'
What shall I call thee?
'I happy am,
Joy is my name.'
Sweet joy befall thee!

Pretty joy!
Sweet joy but two days old,
Sweet joy I call thee:
Thou dost smile,
I sing the while,
Sweet joy befall thee!

# The Lamb

WILLIAM BLAKE

Little Lamb, who made thee?
Dost thou know who made thee?
Gave thee life, and bid thee feed
By the stream and o'er the mead;
Gave thee clothing of delight;
Softest clothing, woolly, bright;
Gave thee such a tender voice,
Making all the vales rejoice?
Little Lamb, who made thee?
Dost thou know who made thee?

Little Lamb, I'll tell thee,
Little Lamb, I'll tell thee:
He is called by thy name,
For he calls himself a Lamb.
He is meek, and he is mild;
He became a little child.
I a child, and thou a lamb,
We are called by His name.
Little Lamb, God bless thee!
Little Lamb, God bless thee!

# from Boswell's Diary

JAMES BOSWELL

## Monday, 9 October 1775

My wife having been seized with her pains in the night,
I got up 'bout three o'clock, and between four and five
Dr Young came. He and I sat upstairs mostly till between
three and four, when, after we had dined, her labour became
violent. I was full of expectation, and meditated curiously
on the thought that it was already certain of what sex the
child was ... I did not feel so much anxiety about my wife
now as on former occasions, better being used to an
inlying. Yet the danger was as great now as ever. I was
easier from the same deception which affects a soldier
who has escaped in several battles. She was very ill.
Between seven and eight I went into the room. She was
just delivered. I heard her say, 'God be thanked for
whatever he sends.' I supposed then that the child was
a daughter. But she herself had not then seen it. Miss
Preston said, 'Is it a daughter?' 'No,' said Mrs Forrest,
the nurse-keeper, 'it's a son.' When I had seen the little
man I said that now I should be so anxious that probably
I should never again have an easy hour. I said to Dr Young
with great seriousness, 'Doctor, Doctor, let no man set
his heart upon anything in this world but lands or heritable
bonds; for he has no security that anything else will last as
long as himself.' My anxiety subdued a flutter of joy which
was in my breast. I wrote several letters to announce my
son's birth. I indulged in some imaginations that he might
perhaps be a great man.

*James Boswell (1740–1795) was a Scottish lawyer and laird.
He is best-known as the friend and biographer of Samuel Johnson but
the publication of his diaries in the 20th century also proved him to be
one of the world's greatest diarists.*

# Life

CHARLOTTE BRONTË

POEM

LIFE, believe, is not a dream
So dark as sages say;
Oft a little morning rain
Foretells a pleasant day.
Sometimes there are clouds of gloom,
But these are transient all;
If the shower will make the roses bloom,
O why lament its fall?

Rapidly, merrily,
Life's sunny hours flit by,
Gratefully, cheerily,
Enjoy them as they fly!

What though Death at times steps in
And calls our Best away?
What though sorrow seems to win,
O'er hope, a heavy sway?
Yet hope again elastic springs,
Unconquered, though she fell;
Still buoyant are her golden wings,
Still strong to bear us well.
Manfully, fearlessly,
The day of trial bear,
For gloriously, victoriously,
Can courage quell despair!

*Charlotte Brontë (1816–1855) was an English writer and eldest of the celebrated Brontë sisters. Charlotte is probably most famous for writing the novels* Jane Eyre *and* Villette. *She also worked as a governess and a school teacher.*

# Tell Me, Tell Me Smiling Child

EMILY BRONTË

Tell me, tell me smiling child
What the past is like to thee?
An Autumn evening soft and mild
With a wind that sighs mournfully.

Tell me what is the present hour?
A green and flowery spray
Where a young bird sits gathering its power
To mount and fly away.

And what is the future happy one?
A sea beneath a cloudless sun
A mighty, glorious dazzling sea
Stretching into infinity.

*Emily Brontë (1818–1848) was one of the famous Brontë sisters. She is probably best known for her novel,* Wuthering Heights, *however, she also wrote many poems but did not receive wide acclaim for her work until after her death.*

# Joy

BUDDHA

Let us live in joy, not hating those who hate us.
Among those who hate us, we live free of hate.
Let us live in joy,
free from disease among those who are diseased.
Among those who are diseased, let us live free of disease.
Let us live in joy, free from greed among the greedy.
Among those who are greedy, we live free of greed.
Let us live in joy, though we possess nothing.
Let us live feeding on joy, like the bright gods.

Victory breeds hate, for the conquered is unhappy.
Whoever has given up victory and defeat is content
and lives joyfully.

There is no fire like lust, no misfortune like hate;
there is no pain like this body;
there is no joy higher than peace.

Craving is the worst disease;
disharmony is the greatest sorrow.
The one who knows this truly knows that nirvana is
the highest bliss.

Health is the greatest gift;
contentment is the greatest wealth;
trusting is the best relationship;
nirvana is the highest joy.

Whoever has tasted the sweetness of solitude and
tranquility becomes free from fear and sin while
drinking the sweetness of the truth.
The sight of the noble is good;
to live with them is always joyful.

Whoever does not see fools will always be happy.
Whoever associates with fools suffers a long time.
Being with fools, as with an enemy, is always painful.

Being with the wise, like meeting with family, is joyful.
Therefore, one should follow the wise, the intelligent,
the learned, the patient, the dutiful, the noble;
one should follow the good and wise,
as the moon follows the path of the stars.

*Siddhartha Buddha  (b. 560 BC) was born a prince in Lumbini,
Nepal. When he was a young man he escaped the palace of his birth
and became the Buddha, the enlightened one, whose teachings of wisdom
and enlightenment were to become the foundations of Buddhism.*

# To Be a Pilgrim
## from The Pilgrim's Progress

JOHN BUNYAN

POEM

Who would true Valour see,
Let him come hither;
One here will Constant be,
Come Wind, come Weather.
There's no Discouragement,
Shall make him once Relent,
His first avow'd Intent,
To be a Pilgrim.

Who so best him round,
With dismal Stories,
Do but themselves Confound;
His Strength the more is.
No Lyon can him fright,
He'll with a Gyant Fight,
But he will have a right,
To be a Pilgrim.

Hobgoblin, nor foul Fiend,
Can daunt his Spirit:
He knows, he at the end,
Shall Life Inherit.
The Fancies fly away,
He'll fear not what men say,
He'll labour Night and Day,
To be a Pilgrim.

*John Bunyan (1628–1688) was a preacher and a prolific
author. His most successful work was* The Pilgrim's Progress
*(1678 and 1684) in which these words were originally found,
although they are now commonly sung as a hymn.*

READING

# I Trust You'll Treat Her Well

VICTOR BUONO

Dear World: I bequeath to you today one little girl ... in a crispy dress ... with two blue eyes ... and a happy laugh that ripples all day long ... and a flash of light blond hair that bounces in the sunlight when she runs. I trust you will treat her well.

She's slipping out of the backyard of my heart this morning ... and skipping off down the street to her first day of school. And never again will she be completely mine. Prim and proud she'll wave her young and independent hand this morning and say 'Goodbye' and walk with little lady steps to the schoolhouse.

Now she'll learn to stand in lines ... and wait by the alphabet for her name to be called. She'll learn to tune her ears for the sounds of school-bells ... and deadlines ... and she'll learn to giggle ... and gossip ... and look at the ceiling in a disinterested way when the little boy across the aisle sticks out his tongue at her. And, now she'll learn to be jealous. And now she'll learn how it is to feel hurt inside. And now she'll learn how not to cry.

No longer will she have time to sit on the front porch steps on a summer day and watch an ant scurry across the crack in the sidewalk. Nor will she have time to pop out of bed with the dawn to kiss lilac blossoms in the morning dew. No, now she will worry about the important things ... like grades and which dress to wear and who's best friend is whose. And the magic of books and learning will replace the magic of her blocks and dolls. And she'll find new heroes.

For five full years now I've been her sage and Santa Claus and pal and playmate and father and friend. Now she'll learn to share her worship with her teachers ... which is only right. But, no longer will I be the smartest, greatest man in the whole world. Today when that school bell rings for the first time ... she'll learn what it means to be a member of the group ... with all its privileges and its disadvantages too.

She'll learn in time that proper young ladies do not laugh out loud ... or kiss dogs ... or keep frogs in pickle jars in bedrooms ... or even watch ants scurry across cracks in sidewalks in the summer.

Today she'll learn for the first time that all who smile at her are not her friends. And I'll stand on the front porch and watch her start out on the long, lonely journey to becoming a woman.

So, world, I bequeath to you one little girl ... in a crispy dress ... with two blue eyes ... and a happy laugh that ripples all day long ... and a flash of light blonde hair that bounces in the sunlight when she runs. I trust you'll treat her well.

*Victor Buono (1938–1982) was a comic actor who always played the villain, the madman or oddball in film, TV and theatre, and returned to the character of Falstaff regularly throughout his life. This fictional letter was read on WHO radio by Van Harden in honour of the first day of school that year.*

POEM

# Rules and Regulations

LEWIS CARROLL

A short direction
To avoid dejection,
By variations
In occupations,
And prolongation
Of relaxation,
And combinations
Of recreations,
And disputation
On the state of the nation
In adaptation
To your station,
By invitations
To friends and relations,
By evitation
Of amputation,
By permutation
In conversation,
And deep reflection
You'll avoid dejection.

Learn well your grammar,
And never stammer,
Write well and neatly,
And sing most sweetly,
Be enterprising,
Love early rising,
Go walk of six miles,
Have ready quick smiles,
With lightsome laughter,
Soft flowing after.
Drink tea, not coffee;
Never eat toffy.
Eat bread with butter.
Once more, don't stutter.
Don't waste your money,
Abstain from honey.
Shut doors behind you,
(Don't slam them, mind you.)
Drink beer, not porter.
Don't enter the water

Till to swim you are able.
Sit close to the table.
Take care of a candle.
Shut a door by the handle,
Don't push with your shoulder
Until you are older.
Lose not a button.
Refuse cold mutton.
Starve your canaries.
Believe in fairies.
If you are able,
Don't have a stable
With any mangers.
Be rude to strangers.

*Moral*: Behave.

*Lewis Carroll (1832–1898) was the pseudonym used by the English author Charles Dodgson for all his writing. His humorous and imaginative writing for children included the classics* Alice's Adventures in Wonderland *and* The Hunting of the Snark. *This is taken from his collection* Useful and Instructive Poetry.

# Into the Future

SYLVIA CHIDI

Into the future
If we could venture
Into the future
We may have a clearer picture
Of if there lie awaiting any hidden rewarding treasures

Somewhere in the scriptures
It is lectured that in our future
We can expect to find torture or pleasure
Perhaps even a mixture of both features

But if we can capture
A moment of our future
I am not sure
We will find any form of closure

For into the future
Is an unpredictable structure
That man itself cannot sculpture
Nor can he take his tape to it and measure

*Sylvia Chidi (b. 1971) is a poet who grew up in Germany
and Nigeria. She now lives and works in England.*

# A Newborn Girl at Passover*

## NAN COHEN

Consider one apricot in a basket of them.
It is very much like all the other apricots –
an individual already, skin and seed.

Now think of this day.  One you will probably forget.
The next breath you take, a long drink of air.
Holiday or not, it doesn't matter.

A child is born and doesn't know what day it is.
The particular joy in my heart she cannot imagine.
The taste of apricots is in store for her.

*Passover is one of the most important religious festivals in
the Jewish calendar. Jews celebrate the Feast of Passover to
commemorate the liberation of the Children of Israel who
were led out of Egypt by Moses.

*Nan Cohen (b. 1968) is a poet who lives in Los Angeles, California.
She is the Poetry Director of the Napa Valley Writers' Conference, a summer
programme that focuses on poetry and fiction.*

# from Frost at Midnight*

SAMUEL TAYLOR COLERIDGE

POEM

Dear Babe, that sleepest cradled by my side,
Whose gentle breathings, heard in this deep calm,
Fill up the interspersed vacancies
And momentary pauses of the thought!
My babe so beautiful! it thrills my heart
With tender gladness, thus to look at thee,
And think that thou shalt learn far other lore,
And in far other scenes! For I was reared
In the great city, pent mid cloisters dim,
And saw nought lovely but the sky and stars.
But thou, my babe! shalt wander like a breeze
By lakes and sandy shores, beneath the crags
Of ancient mountain, and beneath the clouds,
Which image in their bulk both lakes and shores
And mountain crags: so shalt thou see and hear
The lovely shapes and sounds intelligible
Of that eternal language, which thy God
Utters, who from eternity doth teach
Himself in all, and all things in himself.
Great universal Teacher! he shall mould
Thy spirit, and by giving make it ask.

Therefore all seasons shall be sweet to thee,
Whether the summer clothe the general earth
With greenness, or the redbreast sit and sing
Betwixt the tufts of snow on the bare branch
Of mossy apple-tree, while the nigh thatch
Smokes in the sun-thaw; whether the eave-drops fall
Heard only in the trances of the blast,
Or if the secret ministry of frost
Shall hang them up in silent icicles,
Quietly shining to the quiet Moon.

*Samuel Taylor Coleridge composed the poem *Frost at Midnight*
in February 1798.

*Samuel Taylor Coleridge (1772–1834) was a visionary poet. Coleridge's
friendship with poet William Wordsworth was one of the most fruitful relationships
in English literary history and their joint publication of* Lyrical Ballads *in 1798
is seen as the starting point for the English Romantic Movement.*

# Letter to a Godchild
# (To Adam)

SAMUEL TAYLOR COLERIDGE

READING

July 1834

My Dear Godchild,

I offer up the same fervent prayer for you now, as I did
kneeling before the altar, when you were baptized into
Christ, and solemnly received as a living member of
His spiritual body, the Church.

Years must pass before you will be able to read with an
understanding heart what I now write; but I trust that
the all-gracious God, the Father of our Lord Jesus Christ,
the Father of mercies, who, by his only begotten Son,
(all mercies in one sovereign mercy!) has redeemed you
from the evil ground, and willed you to be born out of
darkness, but into light – out of death, but into life –
out of sin, but into righteousness, even into the Lord
our Righteousness; I trust that He will graciously hear
the prayers of your dear parents, and be with you as the
spirit of health and growth in body and mind.

My dear Godchild! – You received from Christ's minister
at the baptismal font, as your Christian name, the name
of a most dear friend of your father's, and who was to me

even as a son, the late Adam Steinmetz, whose fervent aspiration and ever-paramount aim, even from early youth, was to be a Christian in thought, word, and deed – in will, mind, and affections.

I too, your Godfather, have known what the enjoyments and advantages of this life are, and what the more refined pleasures which learning and intellectual power can bestow; and with all the experience which more than threescore years can give, I now, on the eve of my departure, declare to you (and earnestly pray that you may hereafter live and act on the conviction) that health is a great blessing, – competence obtained by honorable industry a great blessing, – and a great blessing it is to have kind, faithful, and loving friends and relatives; but that the greatest of all blessings, as it is the most ennobling of all privileges, is to be indeed a Christian.

# Ode On the Whole Duty of Parents

FRANCES CORNFORD

POEM

The spirits of children are remote and wise,
They must go free
Like fishes in the sea

Or starlings in the skies,
Whilst you remain
The shore where casually they come again.
But when there falls the stalking shade of fear,
You must be suddenly near,
You, the unstable, must become a tree
In whose unending heights of flowering green
Hangs every fruit that grows, with silver bells;
Where heart-distracting magic birds are seen
And all the things a fairy-story tells;
Though still you should possess
Roots that go deep in ordinary earth,
And strong consoling bark
To love and to caress.
Last, when at dark
Safe on the pillow lies an up-gazing head
And drinking holy eyes
Are fixed on you,
When, from behind them, questions come to birth

Insistently,
On all the things that you have ever said
Of suns and snakes and parallelograms and flies,
And whether these are true,

Then for a while you'll need to be no more
That sheltering shore
Or legendary tree in safety spread,
No, then you must put on
The robes of Solomon,
Or simply
be Sir Isaac Newton sitting on the bed.

*Frances Cornford (1886–1960) was a British poet and the granddaughter of the naturalist Charles Darwin. She had five children.*

PRAYER

# A Prayer

JOHN COSIN

Almighty God and heavenly Father,
We thank you for the children which you have given us:
Give us also grace to train them in your faith, fear and love;
That as they advance in years they may grow in grace,
And may hereafter be found in the number of your
elect children;
Through Jesus Christ our Lord.

Amen.

*John Cosin (1594–1672) was an English minister who became Bishop of Durham in 1660. He was greatly involved in the 1662 revision of the Anglican Book of Common Prayer.*

# i thank You God for most this amazing day

E.E. CUMMINGS

i thank You God for most this amazing
day:for the leaping greenly spirits of trees
and a blue true dream of sky;and for everything
which is natural which is infinite which is yes

(i who have died am alive again today,
and this is the sun's birthday;this is the birth
day of life and of love and wings:and of the gay
great happening illimitably earth)

how should tasting touching hearing seeing
breathing any–lifted from the no
of all nothing–human merely being
doubt unimaginable You?

(now the ears of my ears awake and
now the eyes of my eyes are opened)

* The punctuation and spacing used represents the author's
original manuscript.

*E.E. Cummings (1894–1962) was an American poet known for his experimental style. He visually shaped poems, using a unique and personal grammar and by breaking up and putting together words. He often tied this to traditional and romantic subject matter.*

# may my heart always

### E.E. CUMMINGS

may my heart always be open to little
birds who are the secrets of living
whatever they sing is better than to know
and if men should not hear them men are old

may my mind stroll about hungry
and fearless and thirsty and supple
and even if it's Sunday may i be wrong
for whenever men are right they are not young

and may myself do nothing usefully
and love yourself so more than truly
there's never been quite such a fool who could fail
pulling all the sky over him with one smile

\* The punctuation and spacing used represents the author's
original manuscript.

# Learning to Talk

POEM

C. DAY LEWIS

See this small one, tiptoe on
The green foothills of the years,
Views a younger world than yours;
When you go down, he'll be the tall one.

Dawn's dew is on his tongue –
No word for what's behind the sky,
Naming all that meets the eye,
Pleased with sunlight over a lawn.

Hear his laughter. He can't contain
The exquisite moment overflowing.
Limbs leaping, woodpecker flying
Are for him and not hereafter.

Tongue trips, recovers, triumphs,
Turning all ways to express
What the forward eye can guess –
That time is his and earth young.

We are growing too like trees
To give the rising wind a voice:
Eagles shall build upon her verse,
Our winged seeds are tomorrow's sowing.

Yes, we learn to speak for all
Whose hearts here are not at home,
All who march to a better time
And breed the world for which they burn.

Though we fall once, though we often,
Though we fall to rise not again,
From our horizon sons begin;
When we go down, they will be tall ones.

*C. Day Lewis (1904–1972) was a poet and essayist. He was appointed Poet Laureate in 1968 and died just four years later. He was part of a left wing literary set that included W. H. Auden and Stephen Spender (see page 147). His son is the actor Daniel Day Lewis.*

# from Dombey and Son

C H A R L E S   D I C K E N S

Dombey sat in the corner of the darkened room in
the great armchair by the bedside, and Son lay tucked
up warm in a little basket bedstead, carefully disposed
on a low settee immediately in front of the fire and close
to it, as if his constitution were analogous to that of a
muffin, and it was essential to toast him brown while
he was very new.

Dombey was about eight-and-forty years of age. Son
about eight-and-forty minutes. Dombey was rather bald,
rather red, and though a handsome well-made man, too
stern and pompous in appearance, to be prepossessing.
Son was very bald, and very red, and though (of course)
an undeniably fine infant, somewhat crushed and spotty
in his general effect, as yet. On the brow of Dombey, Time
and his brother Care had set some marks, as on a tree that
was to come down in good time – remorseless twins they
are for striding through their human forests, notching as
they go – while the countenance of Son was crossed with
a thousand little creases, which the same deceitful Time
would take delight in smoothing out and wearing away
with the flat part of his scythe, as a preparation of the
surface for his deeper operations.

Dombey, exulting in the long-looked-for event, jingled
and jingled the heavy gold watch-chain that depended from
below his trim blue coat, whereof the buttons sparkled
phosphorescently in the feeble rays of the distant fire. Son,

with his little fists curled up and clenched, seemed, in his feeble way, to be squaring at existence for having come upon him so unexpectedly.

'The House will once again, Mrs Dombey,' said Mr Dombey, 'be not only in name but in fact Dombey and Son;' and he added, in a tone of luxurious satisfaction, with his eyes half-closed as if he were reading the name in a device of flowers, and inhaling their fragrance at the same time; 'Dombey and Son!'...

The earth was made for Dombey and Son to trade in, and the sun and moon were made to give them light. Rivers and seas were formed to float their ships; rainbows gave them promise of fair weather; winds blew for or against their enterprises; stars and planets circled in their orbits, to preserve inviolate a system of which they were the centre. Common abbreviations took new meanings in his eyes, and had sole reference to them.

*Charles Dickens (1812–1870) was one of the foremost novelists of the 19th century, famed for his serialised novels depicting the realities of life in England during the industrial revolution.* Dombey and Son *is seen as Dickens' most domestic novel as it explores redemption through familial love.*

# from Bloomsbury Christening

NOVEL

CHARLES DICKENS

'Now, uncle,' said Mr Kitterbell, lifting up that part of the
mantle which covered the infant's face, with an air of great
triumph, 'WHO do you think he's like?'

'He! he! Yes, who?' said Mrs K., putting her arm through
her husband's, and looking up into Dumps's face with an
expression of as much interest as she was capable of displaying.

'Good God, how small he is!' cried the amiable uncle, starting
back with well-feigned surprise; 'REMARKABLY small indeed.'

'Do you think so?' inquired poor little Kitterbell, rather
alarmed. 'He's a monster to what he was – ain't he, nurse?'

'He's a dear,' said the nurse, squeezing the child, and
evading the question – not because she scrupled to disguise
the fact, but because she couldn't afford to throw away the
chance of Dumps's half-crown.

71

'Well, but who is he like?' inquired little Kitterbell.

Dumps looked at the little pink heap before him, and only
thought at the moment of the best mode of mortifying the
youthful parents.

'I really don't know WHO he's like,' he answered, very
well knowing the reply expected of him.

'Don't you think he's like ME?' inquired his nephew with
a knowing air.

'Oh, DECIDEDLY not!' returned Dumps, with an emphasis
not to be misunderstood. 'Decidedly not like you – Oh,
certainly not.'

'Like Jemima?' asked Kitterbell, faintly.

'Oh, dear no; not in the least. I'm no judge, of course, in
such cases; but I really think he's more like one of those little
carved representations that one sometimes sees blowing

a trumpet on a tombstone!' The nurse stooped down over the child, and with great difficulty prevented an explosion of mirth ...

'Well!' said the disappointed little father, 'you'll be better able to tell what he's like by-and-by. You shall see him this evening with his mantle off.'

'Thank you,' said Dumps, feeling particularly grateful ...

A general hum of admiration interrupted the conversation, and announced the entrance of nurse with the baby. An universal rush of the young ladies immediately took place. (Girls are always SO fond of babies in company.)

'Oh, you dear!' said one.

'How sweet!' cried another, in a low tone of the most enthusiastic admiration.

'Heavenly!' added a third.

'Oh! what dear little arms!' said a fourth, holding up an arm and fist about the size and shape of the leg of a fowl cleanly picked.

'Did you ever!' – said a little coquette with a large bustle, who looked like a French lithograph, appealing to a gentleman in three waistcoats – 'Did you ever!'

'Never, in my life,' returned her admirer, pulling up his collar.

'Oh! DO let me take it, nurse,' cried another young lady. 'The love!'

'Can it open its eyes, nurse?' inquired another, affecting the utmost innocence. – Suffice it to say, that the single ladies unanimously voted him an angel, and that the married ones, agreed that he was decidedly the finest baby they had ever beheld – except their own ...

# In This Short Life

EMILY DICKINSON

POEM

In this short Life
That only lasts an hour
How much -- how little -- is
Within our power

# That Love Is All There Is

EMILY DICKINSON

POEM

That Love is all there is,
Is all we know of Love;
It is enough, the freight should be
Proportioned to the groove.

*Emily Dickinson (1830–1886) was a prolific poet who rarely left her home and seldom socialised. However, her poetry is often characterised by its intimacy, insight, and Dickinson's exploration of her own spirituality.*

NOVEL

# from The Millstone

MARGARET DRABBLE

The midwife asked me if I would like to see the child.
'Please' I said gratefully, and she went away and came
back with my daughter wrapped up in a small grey
bloodstained blanket, and with a ticket saying 'Stacey'
round her ankle. She put her in my arms and I sat there
looking at her, and her great wide blue eyes looked at me
with seeming recognition, and what I felt is pointless to
try and describe. Love, I suppose one might call it, and
the first of my life.

I had expected so little, really. I never expect much. I
had been told of the ugliness of newborn children, of
their red and wrinkled faces, their waxy covering, their
emaciated limbs, their hairy cheeks, their piercing cries.
All I can say is that mine was beautiful and in my defense
I must add that others said she was beautiful too. She was
not red nor even wrinkled, but palely soft, each feature
delicately reposed in its right place, and she was not bald
but adorned with a thick, startling crop of black hair. One
of the nurses fetched a brush and flattened it down and it
covered her forehead, lying in a dense fringe that reached
her eyes. And her eyes, that seemed to see me and that
looked into mine were a profound blue, the whites white
with the gleam of alarming health. When they asked if they
could have her back and put her back into her cradle for the
night, I handed her over without reluctance, for the delight
of holding her was too much for me. I felt as well as they that
such pleasure should be regulated and rationed.

*Margaret Drabble (b. 1939) is an English novelist. This extract
is taken from her novel* The Millstone *(1965) in which a young woman
discovers the love she feels for her illegitimate child whose arrival she
had previously feared.*

74

# Glad of These Times

POEM

HELEN DUNMORE

If you were to reach up your hand,
if you were to push apart the leaves
turning aside your face like one who looks
not at the sun but where the sun hides –
there, where the spider scuttles
and the lizard whips out of sight –

if you were to search
with your small, brown, inexperienced hands
among the leaves that shield the fire of the fruit
in a vault of shadow, if you were to do it
you'd be allowed, for this is your planet
and you are new on it,

if you were to reach inside the leaves
and cup your hands as the fruit descends
like a balloon on the fields of evening
huffing its orange plume
one last time, as the flight ends
and the fruit stops growing –

*Helen Dunmore (b. 1952) is a British novelist, poet, writer and performer who also writes for children. Her novel* A Spell of Winter, *published in 1995, won the first Orange Prize for Fiction.*

SONG

# from Forever Young*

BOB DYLAN

May God bless and keep you always,
May your wishes all come true,
May you always do for others
And let others do for you.
May you build a ladder to the stars
And climb on every rung,
May you stay forever young.

May you grow up to be righteous,
May you grow up to be true,
May you always know the truth
And see the lights surrounding you.
May you always be courageous,
Stand upright and be strong,
May you stay forever young.

May your hands always be busy,
May your feet always be swift,
May you have a strong foundation
When the winds of changes shift.
May your heart always be joyful,
May your song always be sung,
May you stay forever young.

* *Forever Young* was included on Bob Dylan's 1974 album
*Planet Waves* and has become one of his most beloved songs.

*Bob Dylan (b. 1941) is one of the pioneering musicians of
the 20th century. His music is often concerned with the political
and social and his style has ranged over the years from revivalist
folk music to rock.*

## from The Blue Jay's Dance, A Birth Year

LOUISE ERDRICH

Life seems to flood by, taking our lives quickly
in its flow. In the growth of children, in the ageing
of beloved parents, time's chart is magnified,
shown in its particularity, focused, so that with
each celebration of maturity there is also a pang
of loss. This is our human problem, one common
to parents, sons and daughters, too – how to let
go while holding tight, how to simultaneously
cherish the closeness and intricacy of the bond
while at the same time letting out the ravelling
string, the red yarn that ties our hearts.

*Louise Erdrich (b. 1948) is an American writer whose Native American heritage informs much of her writing.* The Blue Jay's Dance, A Birth Year *is, as Erdrich describes it, a 'book about the vitality between mothers and infants, that passionate and artful bond into which we pour the direct expression of our being.'*

POEM

# Riders

ROBERT FROST

The surest thing there is is we are riders,
And though none too successful at it, guiders,
Through everything presented, land and tide
And now the very air, of what we ride.

What is this talked-of mystery of birth
But being mounted bareback on the earth?
We can just see the infant up astride,
His small fist buried in the bushy hide.

There is our wildest mount – a headless horse.
But though it runs unbridled off its course,
And all our blandishments would seem defied,
We have ideas yet that we haven't tried.

*Robert Frost (1874–1963) is beloved for his choice of rural subjects and use of traditional verse form, which is often belied by a powerful, even dark vision. He is recognised as a central figure in the American poetic canon and was awarded the Pulitzer Prize in 1924, 1931, 1937 and 1943.*

# Secret O' Life*

ART GARFUNKEL

The secret of life
Is enjoying the passage of time
Any fool can do it
There ain't nothin' to it
Nobody knows how we got to the top
of the hill
Since we're on our way down
We might as well enjoy the ride

The secret of love
Is in opening up your heart
It's okay to feel afraid
But don't let that stand in your way
'Cause anyone knows
That love is the only road
Since we're only here for awhile

*This song is from Art Garfunkel's album, *Songs from a Parent to a Child*, which was released in 1997.

*Art Garfunkel (b. 1941) is an American singer-songwriter who established his career as one half of the folk band, Simon and Garfunkel.*

# The Birth of Isaac

GENESIS 21:1-8

1 Now the Lord was gracious to Sarah as he had said,
and the Lord did for Sarah what he had promised.

2 Sarah became pregnant and bore a son to Abraham
in his old age, at the very time God had promised him.

3 Abraham gave the name Isaac to the son Sarah
bore him.

4 When his son Isaac was eight days old, Abraham
circumcised him, as God commanded him.

5 Abraham was a hundred years old when his son
Isaac was born to him.

6 Sarah said, 'God has brought me laughter, and
everyone who hears about this will laugh with me'.

7 And she added, 'Who would have said to Abraham
that Sarah would nurse children? Yet I have borne
him a son in his old age'.

8 The child grew and was weaned, and on the day
Isaac was weaned Abraham held a great feast.

*New International Version*

# On Children from The Prophet

KAHLIL GIBRAN

SPIRITUAL

Your children are not your children.
They are the sons and daughters of Life's longing for itself.
They come through you but not from you,
And though they are with you yet they belong not to you.

You may give them your love but not your thoughts,
For they have their own thoughts.
You may house their bodies but not their souls,
For their souls dwell in the house of tomorrow,
which you cannot visit, not even in your dreams.

You may strive to be like them,
but seek not to make them like you.
For life goes not backward nor tarries with yesterday.
You are the bows from which your children as living
arrows are sent forth.
The archer sees the mark upon the path of the infinite,
and He bends you with His might
that His arrows may go swift and far.

*Kahlil Gibran (1883–1931) was a Lebanese philosophical writer, poet and artist renowned for his timeless wisdom. He is seen as having a particular affinity with William Blake, and his work,* The Prophet, *is his most celebrated statement about the truths of human experience.*

# Warning to Children

R O B E R T   G R A V E S

Children, if you dare to think
Of the greatness, rareness, muchness
Fewness of this precious only
Endless world in which you say
You live, you think of things like this:
Blocks of slate enclosing dappled
Red and green, enclosing tawny
Yellow nets, enclosing white
And black acres of dominoes,
Where a neat brown paper parcel
Tempts you to untie the string.
In the parcel a small island,
On the island a large tree,
On the tree a husky fruit.
Strip the husk and pare the rind off:
In the kernel you will see
Blocks of slate enclosed by dappled
Red and green, enclosed by tawny
Yellow nets, enclosed by white
And black acres of dominoes,
Where the same brown paper parcel –
Children, leave the string alone!
For who dares undo the parcel
Finds himself at once inside it,
On the island, in the fruit,

Blocks of slate about his head,
Finds himself enclosed by dappled
Green and red, enclosed by yellow
Tawny nets, enclosed by black
And white acres of dominoes,
With the same brown paper parcel
Still untied upon his knee.
And, if he then should dare to think
Of the fewness, muchness, rareness,
Greatness of this endless only
Precious world in which he says
he lives – he then unties the string.

*Robert Graves (1895–1985) was an English poet as well as a novelist and translator. He is most famous for the poems he wrote behind the lines during the First World War (1914–1918) and his poems about love. He also wrote several collections of poems for children.*

# Baby Feet

EDGAR A. GUEST

Tell me, what is half so sweet
As a baby's tiny feet,
Pink and dainty as can be,
Like a coral from the sea?
Talk of jewels strung in rows,
Gaze upon those little toes,
Fairer than a diadem,
With the mother kissing them!

It is morning and she lies
Uttering her happy cries,
While her little hands reach out
For the feet that fly about.
Then I go to her and blow
Laughter out of every toe;
Hold her high and let her place
Tiny footprints on my face.

Little feet that do not know
Where the winding roadways go,
Little feet that never tire,
Feel the stones or trudge the mire,
Still too pink and still too small
To do anything but crawl,
Thinking all their wanderings fair,
Filled with wonders everywhere.

Little feet, so rich with charm,
May you never come to harm.
As I bend and proudly blow
Laughter out of every toe,
This pray, that God above
Shall protect you with His love,
And shall guide those little feet
Safely down life's broader street.

85

*Edgar A. Guest (1881–1959) was a British-born American writer who wrote daily poems in the* Detroit Free Press. *These became so popular that they were eventually syndicated to newspapers throughout the country and Guest became a household name.*

POEM

# Holy Baptism (II)*

GEORGE HERBERT

Since, Lord, to thee
A narrow way and little gate
Is all the passage, on my infancy
Thou didst lay hold, and antedate
My faith in me.

O let me still
Write thee great God, and me a child:
Let me be soft and supple to thy will,
Small to myself, to others mild,
Behither ill.

Although by stealth
My flesh get on: yet let her sister
My soul bid nothing, but preserve her wealth:
The growth of flesh is but a blister;
Childhood is health.

\* This is the second of two poems that George Herbert wrote
entitled 'Holy Baptism'.

*George Herbert (1593–1633) was a metaphysical poet and a clergyman.
His poems celebrate the many aspects of God's love as he discovered them and
yet, despite their religious subject, Herbert's quiet intensity and examination of
human existence mean they are relevant to the most secular of readers.*

# Full Moon and Little Frieda

TED HUGHES

A cool small evening shrunk to a dog bark and the
   clank of a bucket –

And you listening.
A spider's web, tense for the dew's touch.
A pail lifted, still and brimming – mirror
To tempt a first star to a tremor.

Cows are going home in the lane there, looping the
   hedges with their warm wreaths of breath –
A dark river of blood, many boulders,
Balancing unspilled milk.

'Moon!' you cry suddenly, 'Moon! Moon!'
The moon has stepped back like an artist gazing
   amazed at a work
That points at him amazed.

*Ted Hughes (1930–1998) who was made English Poet Laureate in
1984, is known for his almost primitive poetry that often focuses on the
natural world. This poem refers to his young daughter, Frieda, one of two
children he and his first wife, the poet Sylvia Plath, had together.*

# To the House of Jacob

ISAIAH 46:3-4

3 'Listen to me, O house of Jacob,
  all you who remain of the house of Israel,
  you whom I have upheld since you were conceived,
  and have carried since your birth.'
4 Even to your old age and grey hairs
  I am he, I am he who will sustain you.
  I have made you and I will carry you;
  I will sustain you and I will rescue you.'

88

# Letter to the Exiles

JEREMIAH 29:11

11 'For I know the plans I have for you,' declares
  the LORD, 'plans to prosper you and not to
  harm you, plans to give you hope and a future.'

*New International Version*

# It Is Not Growing Like a Tree

POEM

BEN JONSON

It is not growing like a tree
In bulk doth make Man better be;
Or standing long an oak, three hundred year,
To fall a log at last, dry, bald, and sere:
A lily of a day
Is fairer far in May,
Although it fall and die that night –
It was the plant and flower of light.
In small proportions we just beauties see;
And in short measures life may perfect be.

89

*Ben Jonson (1572–1637) was a leading Jacobean playwright, known for his satirical and witty comedies such as* Volpone. *He was part of a group of writers who gathered at the Mermaid tavern in Cheapside, London, where he had a great influence on younger poets and writers.*

# Salutation to the Dawn

KALIDASA

Look to this day!
For it is life, the very life of life.
In its brief course
Lie all the verities and realities of your existence:
The bliss of growth;
The glory of action;
The splendour of achievement;
For yesterday is but a dream,
And tomorrow is only a vision;
But today, well lived, makes every yesterday
a dream of happiness,
And every tomorrow a vision of hope.

*Kalidasa (believed to have lived sometime during the 4th and 5th centuries BC) was an Indian Sanskrit dramatist and poet, but little is known about his life, and where and when he lived. His writings are based mainly on Hindu mythology and philosophy.*

# from Letter to Daniel

FERGAL KEANE

Hong Kong, February 1996

My dear son, it is six o'clock in the morning on the
island of Hong Kong. You are asleep cradled in my
left arm and I am learning the art of one-handed typing.
Your mother, more tired yet more happy than I've ever
known her, is sound asleep in the room next door and
there is a soft quiet in our apartment.

Since you've arrived, days have melted into night
and back again and we are learning a new grammar,
a long sentence whose punctuation marks are feeding
and winding and nappy changing and these occasional
moments of quiet.

When you're older we'll tell you that you were born in
Britain's last Asian colony in the lunar year of the pig
and that when we brought you home, the staff of our
apartment block gathered to wish you well. 'It's a boy,
so lucky, so lucky. We Chinese love boys,' they told us.
One man said you were the first baby to be born in the
block in the year of the pig. This, he told us, was good
Feng Shui, in other words a positive sign for the building
and everyone who lived there.

Naturally your mother and I were only too happy to
believe that. We had wanted you and waited for you,
imagined you and dreamed about you and now that you
are here no dream can do justice to you. Outside the
window, below us on the harbour, the ferries are
ploughing back and forth to Kowloon. Millions are
already up and moving about and the sun is slanting
through the tower blocks and out on to the flat silver
waters of the South China Sea. I can see the trail of a
jet over Lamma Island and, somewhere out there, the
last stars flickering towards the other side of the world.

We have called you Daniel Patrick but I've been told
by my Chinese friends that you should have a Chinese
name as well and this glorious dawn sky makes me
think we'll call you Son of the Eastern Star. So that
later, when you and I are far from Asia, perhaps
standing on a beach some evening, I can point at
the sky and tell you of the Orient and the times
and the people we knew there in the last years of
the twentieth century.

Your coming has turned me upside down and inside out.
So much that seemed essential to me has, in the past few
days, taken on a different colour. Like many foreign
correspondents I know, I have lived a life that, on occasion,
has veered close to the edge: war zones, natural disasters,
darkness in all its shapes and forms.

In a world of insecurity and ambition and ego, it's
easy to be drawn in, to take chances with our lives,
to believe that what we do and what people say about
us is reason enough to gamble with death. Now, looking
at your sleeping face, inches away from me, listening
to your occasional sigh and gurgle, I wonder how I
could have ever thought glory and prizes and praise
were sweeter than life.

*Fergal Keane (b. 1961) was based in Hong Kong as the BBC's Asia
correspondent at the time he wrote this reflection on the world into which his
newborn son, Daniel Patrick Keane, had entered.*

# To a Child

CHARLES KINGSLEY

My fairest child, I have no song to sing thee;
No lark could pipe in skies so dull and grey;
Yet, if thou wilt, one lesson I will give thee
For every day.
Be good, sweet maid, and let who can be clever;
Do lovely things, not dream them, all day long;
And so make Life, Death, and that vast For Ever
One grand sweet song.

*Charles Kingsley (1819–1875) was an English minister, Christian Socialist and novelist who also wrote poetry and political articles. However, he is most famous for his classic children's book,* The Water Babies, *which he wrote for his son Grenville in 1862.*

# If

RUDYARD KIPLING

POEM

If you can keep your head when all about you
Are losing theirs and blaming it on you;
If you can trust yourself when all men doubt you,
But make allowance for their doubting too:
If you can wait and not be tired by waiting,
Or, being lied about, don't deal in lies,
Or being hated don't give way to hating,
And yet don't look too good, nor talk too wise;

If you can dream and not make dreams your master;
If you can think and not make thoughts your aim,
If you can meet with Triumph and Disaster
And treat those two impostors just the same:
If you can bear to hear the truth you've spoken
Twisted by knaves to make a trap for fools,
Or watch the things you gave your life to, broken,
And stoop and build'em up with worn-out tools;

If you can make one heap of all your winnings
And risk it on one turn of pitch-and-toss,
And lose, and start again at your beginnings,
And never breathe a word about your loss:
If you can force your heart and nerve and sinew
To serve your turn long after they are gone,
And so hold on when there is nothing in you
Except the Will which says to them: 'Hold on!'

95

If you can talk with crowds and keep your virtue,
Or walk with Kings – nor lose the common touch,
If neither foes nor loving friends can hurt you,
If all men count with you, but none too much:
If you can fill the unforgiving minute
With sixty seconds' worth of distance run,
Yours is the Earth and everything that's in it,
And – which is more – you'll be a Man, my son!

*Rudyard Kipling (1865–1936) was a prolific English poet and author who wrote the children's classics,* The Jungle Book, Just So Stories *and* Kim. *'If', with its themes of self-control and stoicism, is one of Kipling's most famous poems.*

# The Children's Song

POEM

RUDYARD KIPLING

Land of our Birth, we pledge to thee
Our love and toil in the years to be;
When we are grown and take our place
As men and women with our race.

Father in Heaven who lovest all,
Oh, help Thy children when they call;
That they may build from age to age
An undefiled heritage.

Teach us to bear the yoke in youth,
With steadfastness and careful truth;
That, in our time, Thy Grace may give
The Truth whereby the Nations live.

Teach us to rule ourselves alway,
Controlled and cleanly night and day;
That we may bring, if need arise,
No maimed or worthless sacrifice.

Teach us to look in all our ends
On Thee for judge, and not our friends;
That we, with Thee, may walk uncowed
By fear or favour of the crowd.

Teach us the Strength that cannot seek,
By deed or thought, to hurt the weak;
That, under Thee, we may possess
Man's strength to comfort man's distress.

Teach us Delight in simple things,
And Mirth that has no bitter springs;
Forgiveness free of evil done,
And Love to all men 'neath the sun!

Land of our Birth, our faith, our pride,
For whose dear sake our fathers died;
Oh, Motherland, we pledge to thee
Head, heart and hand through the years to be!

# Choosing a Name

CHARLES AND MARY LAMB

I have got a new-born sister:
I was nigh the first that kissed her.
When the nursing-woman brought her
To papa, his infant daughter,
How papa's dear eyes did glisten!
She will shortly be to christen;
And papa has made the offer,
I shall have the naming of her.

Now I wonder what would please her, –
Charlotte, Julia, or Louisa?
Ann and Mary, they're too common;
Joan's too formal for a woman;
Jane's a prettier name beside;
But we had a Jane that died.
They would say, if 'twas Rebecca,
That she was a little Quaker.
Edith's pretty, but that looks
Better in old English books;
Ellen's left off long ago;
Blanche is out of fashion now.
None that I have named as yet
Is so good as Margaret.

Emily is neat and fine;
What do you think of Caroline?
How I'm puzzled and perplexed
What to choose or think of next!
I am in a little fever
Lest the name that I should give her
Should disgrace her or defame her; –
I will leave papa to name her.

*Charles Lamb (1775–1834)* **and** *Mary Lamb (1765–1847)* **were**
*the brother and sister best known for writing* Tales from Shakespeare,
*a collection of prose adaptations of Shakespeare's verse for children.*
*This poem is from their collaborative collection* Poetry for Children.

## from the Tao Te Ching (1)

LAO TZU

The Tao gives birth to all of creation.
The virtue of Tao in nature nurtures them,
and their family gave them their form.
Their environment then shapes them into completion.
That is why every creature honours the Tao and its virtue.

No one tells them to honour the Tao and its virtue,
it happens all by itself.
So the Tao gives them birth,
and its virtue cultivates them,
cares for them,
nurtures them,
gives them a place of refuge and peace,
helps them to grow and shelters them.

It gives them life without wanting to possess them,
and cares for them expecting nothing in return.
It is their master, but does not seek to dominate them.
This is called the dark and mysterious virtue.

## from the Tao Te Ching (2)

LAO TZU

Giving birth and nourishing, having without possessing,
acting with no expectations, leading and not trying to
control: this is the supreme virtue.

*Lao Tzu (lived c.600 BC) was a Chinese Taoist philosopher and is attributed
with writing the* Tao Te Ching *(tao means 'the way of all life,' te means 'the fit use
of life by men,' and* ching *means 'text' or 'classic'). He believed that peoples'
behaviour should be governed by instinct and their conscience.*

POEM

# Born Yesterday

PHILIP LARKIN

Tightly-folded bud,
I have wished you something
None of the others would:
Not the usual stuff
About being beautiful,
Or running off a spring
Of innocence and love –
They will all wish you that,
And should it prove possible,
Well, you're a lucky girl.

But if it shouldn't, then
May you be ordinary;
Have, like other women,
An average of talents:
Not ugly, not good-looking,
Nothing uncustomary
To pull you off your balance,
That, unworkable itself,
Stops all the rest from working.
In fact, may you be dull –
If that is what a skilled,
Vigilant, flexible,
Unemphasized, enthralled
Catching of happiness is called.

*Philip Larkin (1922–1985) was a poet, novelist, librarian and jazz critic. Larkin himself feared marriage and family but this poem reveals a sensitive understanding of the joys of new life and parenthood.*

# from The Rainbow

NOVEL

D.H. LAWRENCE

... He saw the joy coming. He saw the lovely, creamy, cool
little ear of the baby, a bit of dark hair rubbed to a bronze
floss, like bronze dust. And he waited for the child to
become his, to look at him and answer him.

It had a separate being, but it was his own child. His
flesh and blood vibrated to it. He caught the baby to
his breast with his passionate, clapping laugh. And the
infant knew him.

As the newly-opened, newly-dawned eyes looked at
him, he wanted them to perceive him, to recognize him.
Then he was verified. The child knew him, a queer contortion
came on its face for him. He caught it to his breast, clapping
with a triumphant laugh.

It began to be strong, to move vigorously and freely,
to make sounds like words. It was a baby girl now. Already
it knew his strong hands, it exulted in his strong clasp,
it laughed and crowed when he played with it ...

... So Ursula became the child of her father's heart. She
was the little blossom, he was the sun. He was patient,
energetic, inventive for her. He taught her all the funny
little things, he filled her and roused her to her fullest tiny
measure. She answered him with her extravagant infant's
laughter and her call of delight.

*D.H. Lawrence (1885–1930) explored themes of human love and
desire for survival by three generations of the Brangwen family in his novel*
The Rainbow. *His novels are often concerned with human emotions and
consciousness and have provoked both sharp criticism and deep respect.*

# from The Firstborn

LAURIE LEE

... Here she is then, my daughter, here, alive, the one I must possess and guard. A year ago this space was empty, not even a hope of her was in it. Now she's here, brand new, with our name upon her: and no one will call in the night to reclaim her.

She is here for good, her life stretching before us, twenty-odd years wrapped up in that bundle; she will grow, learn to totter, to run in the garden, run back, and call this place home. Or will she?

... As it is, my daughter is so new to me still that I can't yet leave her alone. I have to keep on digging her out of her sleep to make sure that she's really alive.

She is a time-killing lump, her face a sheaf of masks which she shuffles through aimlessly. One by one she reveals them, while I watch eerie rehearsals of those emotions she will one day need; random, out-of-sequence but already exact, automatic but strangely knowing – a quick pucker of fury, a puff of ho-hum boredom, a beaming after-dinner smile, perplexity, slyness, a sudden wrinkling of grief, pop-eyed interest, and fat-lipped love.

It is little more than a month since I was handed this living heap of expectations, and I can feel nothing but simple awe.

What have I got exactly? And what am I going to do with her? And what for that matter will she do with me?

I have got a daughter, whose life is already separate from mine, whose will already follows its own directions, and who has quickly corrected my woolly preconceptions of her by being something remorselessly different. She is the child of herself and what she will be. I am merely the keeper of her temporary helplessness.

Even so, with luck, she can alter me; indeed, is doing so now. At this stage in my life she will give me more than she gets, and may even later become my keeper.

But if I could teach her anything at all – by unloading upon her some of the ill-tied parcels of my years – I'd like it to be acceptance and a holy relish for life. To accept with gladness the fact of being a woman – when she'll find all nature to be on her side.

*Laurie Lee (1914–1997) was a much-loved English poet, novelist and screenwriter. In* The Firstborn *he described the birth of his first daughter, Jesse, after 12 years of marriage.*

POEM

# To a May Baby

WINIFRED LETTS

To come at tulip time how wise!
Perhaps you will not now regret
The shining gardens, jewel set,
Of your first home in Paradise
Nor fret
Because you might not quite forget.

To come at swallow-time how wise!
When every bird has built a nest;
Now you may fold your wings and rest
And watch this new world with surprise;
A guest
For whom the earth has donned her best.

To come when life is gay how wise!
With lambs and every happy thing
That frisks on foot or sports on wing,
With daisies and with butterflies,
But Spring
Had nought so sweet as you to bring.

*Winifred Letts (1882–1972) was an Irish poet, novelist and
playwright who often wrote about folk life and Irish peasantry.*

# from Letter to His Son's Headmaster

## ABRAHAM LINCOLN

... He will have to learn, I know, that all men are not just, all men are not true. But teach him also that for every scoundrel there is a hero, that for every selfish politician, there is a dedicated leader. Teach him that for every enemy, there is a friend. It will take him time I know. But teach him if you can that a dollar earned is of far more value than five pounds. Teach him to learn to lose. And also to enjoy winning. Steer him away from envy, if you can, teach him the secret of quiet laughter. Let him learn easily that the bullies are the easiest to lick. Teach him if you can, the wonder of books. But also give him quiet time to ponder the eternal mystery of birds in the sky, bees in the sun, and flowers on a green hillside. In school, teach him it is far more honourable to fail than to cheat. Teach him to have faith in his own ideas, even if everyone tells him they are wrong. Teach him to be gentle with gentle people, and tough with the tough. Try to give my son the strength not to follow the crowd, when everyone is getting on the bandwagon. Teach him to listen to all men. But teach him also to filter all he hears on a screen of truth, and take only the good that comes through. Teach him if you can how to laugh when he is sad. Teach him there is no shame is tears. Teach him to scoff at cynics and to beware of too much sweetness. Teach him to sell his brawn and brain to the highest bidders, but never to put a price tag on his heart and soul. Teach him to close his ears to a howling mob, and to stand and fight if he thinks he is right. Treat him gently, but do not cuddle him, because only the test of fire makes fine steel. Let him have the courage to be impatient. Let him have the patience to be brave. Teach him always to have sublime faith in himself because then he will always have sublime faith in mankind. This is a big order but see what you can do. He is such a fine fellow, my son!

*Abraham Lincoln (1809–1865) was the President of the United States between 1861 and 1865. He brought about the emancipation of slaves in America and preserved the Union during the American Civil War. This letter was written to the headmaster of his son's school and has become a reference for many parents.*

# Children

HENRY WADSWORTH LONGFELLOW

POEM

Come to me, O ye children!
For I hear you at your play,
And the questions that perplexed me
Have vanished quite away.

Ye open the eastern windows
That look towards the sun,
Where thoughts are singing swallows
And the brooks of morning run.

In your hearts are the birds and the sunshine,
In your thoughts the brooklet's flow,
But in mine is the wind of Autumn
And the first fall of the snow.

Ah! What would the world be to us
If the children were no more?
We should dread the desert behind us
Worse than the dark before.

What the leaves are to the forest,
With light and air for food,
Ere their sweet and tender juices
Have been hardened into wood, –

That to the world are children;
Through them it feels the glow
Of a brighter and sunnier climate
Than reaches the trunks below.

Come to me, O ye children!
And whisper in my ear
What the birds and the winds are singing
In your sunny atmosphere.

For what are all our contrivings,
And the wisdom of your books,
When compared with your caresses,
And the gladness of your looks?

Ye are better than all the ballads
That were ever sung or said;
For ye are living poems,
And all the rest are dead.

*Henry Wadsworth Longfellow (1807–1882)* was one of the most popular American poets of his lifetime, and his use of allegory and easy rhyme characterize many of his poems. One of his most famous works is 'The Song of Hiawatha'.

# Baby

G E O R G E   M A C D O N A L D

Where did you come from, baby dear?
Out of the everywhere into the here.

Where did you get those eyes so blue?
Out of the sky as I came through.

What makes the light in them sparkle and spin?
Some of the starry spikes left in.

Where did you get that little tear?
I found it waiting when I got here.

What makes your forehead so smooth and high?
A soft hand strok'd it as I went by.

What makes your cheek like a warm white rose?
I saw something better than any one knows.

Whence that three-corner'd smile of bliss?
Three angels gave me at once a kiss.

Where did you get this pearly ear?
God spoke, and it came out to hear.

Where did you get those arms and hands?
Love made itself into bonds and bands.

Feet, whence did you come, you darling things?
From the same box as the cherubs' wings.

How did they all just come to be you?
God thought about me, and so I grew.

But how did you come to us, you dear?
God thought about you, and so I am here.

*George MacDonald* (1824–1905) *was a Scottish poet, novelist and clergyman best known for the children's books* The Princess and the Goblin *and* The Princess and Curdy. *His allegorical fairy tales have delighted both children and adults.*

# When I Was Christened

POEM

DAVID MCCORD

When I was christened
they help me up
and poured some water
out of a cup.

The trouble was
it fell on me,
and I and water
don't agree.

A lot of christeners
stood and listened:
I let them know
that I was christened.

*David McCord (1897–1997) was an American poet who often wrote for children and was known for his creative, rhythmic and often whimsical poetry.*

# Songbird

CHRISTINE MCVIE

For you there'll be no crying
For you the sun will be shining
'Cause I feel that when I'm with you
It's alright, I know it's right

And the songbirds keep singing
Like they know the score
And I love you, I love you, I love you
Like never before

To you, I would give the world
To you, I'd never be cold
'Cause I feel that when I'm with you
It's alright, I know it's right

And the songbirds keep singing
Like they know the score
And I love you, I love you, I love you
Like never before

Like never before; like never before.

*Christine McVie (b. 1943) is an English-born singer, songwriter and keyboard player who was part of the British/American rock band Fleetwood Mac. 'Songbird', which appears on Fleetwood Mac's album* Rumours, *became even more famous when it was performed by the American singer Eva Cassidy.*

# from a Speech Given at the
# Campaign to Make Poverty History*

NELSON MANDELA

... as long as poverty, injustice and gross inequality persist in our world, none of us can truly rest ... Massive poverty and obscene inequality are such terrible scourges of our times – times in which the world boasts breathtaking advances in science, technology, industry and wealth accumulation – that they have to rank alongside slavery and apartheid as social evils.

... Like slavery and apartheid, poverty is not natural. It is man-made and it can be overcome and eradicated by the actions of human beings. And overcoming poverty is not a gesture of charity. It is an act of justice. It is the protection of a fundamental human right, the right to dignity and a decent life. While poverty persists, there is no true freedom.

... Sometimes it falls upon a generation to be great. You can be that great generation. Let your greatness blossom. Of course the task will not be easy. But not to do this would be a crime against humanity, against which I ask all humanity now to rise up.

*On 3 February 2005, Nelson Mandela gave this speech to a crowd of thousands in Trafalgar Square, London, at the Make Poverty History campaign's first mass rally.

*Nelson Mandela (b. 1918) led the civil rights struggle against apartheid in South Africa for many years and was imprisoned between 1964 and 1990, where he became a symbol of black resistance. He retired from active politics in 1999. He won the Nobel Peace Prize in 1993 for his humanitarian work.*

BIBLICAL

# The Little Children and Jesus

MARK 10:13–16

13 People were bringing little children to Jesus to have
him touch them, but the disciples rebuked them.

14 When Jesus saw this, he was indignant. He said
to them, 'Let the little children come to me, and
do not hinder them, for the kingdom of God
belongs to such as these.

15 I tell you the truth, anyone who will not receive
the kingdom of God like a little child will never
enter it.'

16 And he took the children in his arms, put his hands
on them, and blessed them.

*New International Version*

# There Is a Song in Man

SPIKE MILLIGAN

POEM

There is a song in man
There is a song in woman
And that is the child's song.
When that song comes
There will be no words.
Do not ask where they are.
Just listen to the song.
Listen to it –
Learn it –
It is the greatest song of all.

*Spike Milligan (1918–2002) was an English writer, poet and comic. He began writing poetry to help him cope with periods of depression. As well as writing serious poetry, he also wrote funny poems and nonsense rhymes.*

POEM

# To My Daughter Jane

SPIKE MILLIGAN

I cannot tell you in words,
I cannot tell you in sounds,
I cannot tell you in music
How much I love you.
I can only tell you in trees,
In mountains,
Oceans,
Streams.
I might be heard to say it
In the bark of a seal on moon misty nights.
It can be heard on the hinges of dawn.
Tho' my music is slain,
All else says I love you Jane.

# The Christening

A.A. MILNE

What shall I call
My dear little dormouse?
His eyes are small,
But his tail is e-nor-mouse.

I sometimes call him Terrible John,
'Cos his tail goes on –
And on –
And on.

And I sometimes call him Terrible Jack,
'Cos his tail goes on to the end of his back.
And I sometimes call him Terrible James,
'Cos he says he likes me calling him names ...

But I think I shall call him Jim,
'Cos I am fond of him.

*A.A. Milne (1892–1956) was a humourist and playwright. He is probably best known for creating the characters Winnie the Pooh and Christopher Robin.*

POEM

# Beattie is Three

ADRIAN MITCHELL

At the top of the stairs
I ask for her hand. O.K.
She gives it to me.
How her fist fits my palm.

A bunch of consolation.
We take our time
Down the steep carpetway
As I wish silently
That the stairs were endless.

*Adrian Mitchell (1932–2008) was a playwright, novelist and poet. He wrote for both adults and children, but increasingly spent time writing for children, with his six grandchildren in mind.*

# Wishes to Welcome Two New Babies

ADRIAN MITCHELL

(for Zoe and Lola)

the milk of the moon
the wine of the sun
the friendship of grass
and salty sand

adventures with Jumblies
and Peter Rabbit
and all the daft creatures
of Wonderland

Paul, Ringo,
George and John
bless the floors
you dance upon

elephant rides
affectionate apes
and the sheep and rocks
of mountainside farms

a cat which will curl
round your neck like a scarf
and a golden retriever
to lie in your arms

I wish you wild happy and gentle sad
and all the love of your Mum and Dad.

# from a Letter to the
# Countess of Bute

LADY MARY WORTLEY MONTAGU

28 January 1753

You should encourage your daughter to talk over with
you what she reads; and as you are very capable of
distinguishing, take care she does not mistake pert
folly for wit and humour, or rhyme for poetry, which
are the common errors of young people, and have a
train of ill consequences. The second caution to be
given her (and which is most absolutely necessary)
is to conceal whatever learning she attains, with as
much solicitude as she would hide crookedness of
lameness: the parade of it can only serve to draw on
her the envy, and consequently the most inveterate
hatred, of all he and she fools, which will certainly
be at least three parts in four of her acquaintance.
The use of knowledge in our sex, beside the amusement
of solitude, is to moderate the passions, and learn to
be contented with small expense, which are the certain
effects of a studious life: and it may be preferable even
to that fame which men have engrossed to themselves,
and will not suffer us to share. You will tell me I have
not observed this rule myself; but you are mistaken:
it is only inevitable accident that has given me any
reputation that way. I have always carefully avoided it,
and ever thought it a misfortune. The explanation of

this paragraph would occasion a long digression, which I will not trouble you with, it being my present design only to say what I think useful for the instruction of my granddaughter, which I have much at heart, If she has the same inclination (I should say passion) for learning that I was born with, history, geography and philosophy will furnish her with materials to pass away cheerfully a longer life that is allotted to mortals. I believe there are few heads capable of making Sir Isaac Newton's calculations, but the result of them is not difficult to be understood by a moderate capacity.

*Lady Mary Wortley Montagu (1689–1762) is remembered as an essayist, poet, letter writer, traveller and eccentric. She wrote regularly to her daughter, the Countess of Bute, and her complete letters were published in the 20th century.*

# You Are So Beautiful

KRIS MORRIS

You are so beautiful
I'll watch over you every night

You are so beautiful
You wake me every morning with a smile

You are so beautiful
I'll work hard I will provide

You are so beautiful
You've captured my heart set it alight

I was not prepared for what you'd do to me
I have so much love for you,
I'll always be here

You are so beautiful
the kindest little heart I've ever seen

You are so beautiful
I'll sing you lullabies as you dream

You are so beautiful
I'll hold you close, never let you go

You are so beautiful
I'll sing it over till you know

124

*Kris Morris (b. 1976) was born just north of Sydney, Australia, and is a singer-songwriter who now lives in London, England. This song was written for his baby daughter, Ruby Rose, and appears on his debut album.*

# To My Children

POEM

S A R O J I N I   N A I D U

Jaya Surya

Golden sun of victory, born
In my life's unclouded morn,
In my lambent sky of love,
May your growing glory prove
Sacred to your consecration,
To my heart and to my nation.
Sun of victory, may you be
Sun of song and liberty.

Padmaja

Lotus-maiden, you who claim
All the sweetness of your name,
Lakshmi, fortune's queen, defend you,
Lotus-born like you, and send you
Balmy moons of love to bless you,
Gentle joy-winds to caress you.
Lotus-maiden, may you be
Fragrant of all ecstasy.

Ranadheera

Little lord of battle, hail
In your newly-tempered mail!
Learn to conquer, learn to fight
In the foremost flanks of right,

Like Valmiki's heroes bold,
Rubies girt in epic gold.
Lord of battle, may you be,
Lord of love and chivalry.

Lilamani

Limpid jewel of delight
Severed from the tender night
Of your sheltering mother-mine,
Leap and sparkle, dance and shine,
Blithely and securely set
In love's magic coronet.
Living jewel, may you be
Laughter-bound and sorrow-free.

*Sarojini Naidu (1879–1949) was the first Indian woman to become President of the Indian National Congress and an Indian state governor. She was also a feminist and a poet, and caused a scandal by marrying a man who wasn't from her Hindu caste. This poem is written to her four children.*

# Baby's Birthday

EDITH NESBITT

G.T.A.

Before your life that is to come,
Love stands with eager eyes, that vainly
Seek to discern what gift may fit
The slow unfolding years of it;
And still Time's lips are sealed and dumb,
And still Love sees no future plainly.

We cannot guess what flowers will spring
Best in your garden, bloom most brightly;
But some fair flowers in any plot
Will spring and grow, and wither not;
And such wish-flowers we gladly bring,
And in that small hand lay them lightly.

Baby, we wish that those dear eyes
May see fulfillment of our dreaming,
Those little feet may turn from wrong,
Those hands to hold the right be strong,
That heart be pure, that mind be wise
To know the true from true-seeming.

We wish that all your life may be
A life of selfless brave endeavour –
That for reward the fates allow
Such love as lines your soft nest now
To warm the years for you, when we,
Who wish you this, are cold for ever.

*Edith Nesbitt (1858–1924) was an English writer who began her literary career by writing verse, but is best known for her successful children's stories. She took a keen interest in socialism and in 1883 was one of the founders of the 'Fellowship of New Life', from which sprang the Fabian Society in London.*

POEM

# Give Yourself a Hug

GRACE NICHOLS

Give yourself a hug
when you feel unloved

Give yourself a hug
when people put on airs
to make you feel a bug

Give yourself a hug
when everyone seems to give you
a cold-shoulder shrug

Give yourself a hug –
a big big hug

And keep on singing,
'Only one in a million like me
Only one in a million-billion-thrillion-zillion
like me.'

*Grace Nichols (b. 1950) was born in Guyana and trained as a teacher and journalist there before immigrating to Britain in 1977. Her poetry, which is inspired by her Caribbean heritage, is lyrical and honest, with a natural rhythm.*

# Children Learn What They Live

POEM

DOROTHY LAW NOLTE

If children live with criticism, they learn to condemn.
If children live with hostility, they learn to fight.
If children live with fear, they learn to be apprehensive.
If children live with pity, they learn to feel sorry for themselves.
If children live with ridicule, they learn to feel shy.
If children live with jealousy, they learn to feel envy.
If children live with shame, they learn to feel guilty.

If children live with encouragement, they learn confidence.
If children live with tolerance, they learn patience.
If children live with praise, they learn appreciation.
If children live with acceptance, they learn to love.
If children live with approval, they learn to like themselves.
If children live with recognition, they learn it is good
   to have a goal.

If children live with sharing, they learn generosity.
If children live with honesty, they learn truthfulness.
If children live with fairness, they learn justice.
If children live with kindness and consideration, they
   learn respect.
If children live with security, they learn to have faith in
   themselves and in those about them.
If children live with friendliness, they learn the world is
   a nice place in which to live.

*Dorothy Law Nolte (1924–2005) was an American author. She wrote this poem in 1954 for her column on raising a family that she wrote for the southern Californian weekly newspaper, the* Torrance Herald*. It has since been translated into more than 35 languages, and adapted into many different versions.*

PRAYER

# In Thy Journeys To and Fro

## TIMOTHY OLUFOSOYE

In thy journeys to and fro
God direct thee;
In thy happiness and pleasure
God bless thee;
In care, anxiety or trouble
God sustain thee;
In peril and in danger
God protect thee.

*Timothy Olufosoye (1918–1992) was born in Nigeria and became the first archbishop and primate of the Church of Nigeria, which is part of the Anglican Communion, in 1979.*

# Sara In Her Father's Arms

POEM

GEORGE OPPEN

Cell by cell the baby made herself, the cells
Made cells. That is to say
The baby is made largely of milk. Lying in her father's arms,
the little seed eyes
Moving, trying to see, smiling for us
To see, she will make a household
To her need of these rooms – Sara, little seed,
Little violent, diligent seed. Come let us look at the world
Glittering: this seed will speak,
Max, words! There will be no other words in the world
But those our children speak. What will she make of a world
Do you suppose, Max, of which she is made.

*George Oppen (1908–1984) is an American poet. He wrote this poem to his friend, Max, after the birth of Max's daughter, Sara.*

POEM

# A Wish for My Children

### EVANGELINE PATERSON

On this doorstep I stand
year after year
to watch you going

and think: May you not
skin your knees. May you
not catch your fingers
in car doors. May
your hearts not break.

May tide and weather
wait for your coming

and may you grow strong
to break
all webs of my weaving.

*Evangeline Paterson (b. 1948) was identified as one of a significant group of poets in a 1988 poetry anthology called* The New British Poetry. *In the 1970s, she co-founded the Durham-based magazine* Other Poetry, *with Anne Stevenson.*

# You're

SYLVIA PLATH

POEM

Clownlike, happiest on your hands,
Feet to the stars, and moon-skulled,
Gilled like a fish. A common-sense
Thumbs-down on the dodo's mode.
Wrapped up in yourself like a spool,
Trawling your dark, as owls do.
Mute as a turnip from the Fourth
Of July to All Fools' Day,
O high-riser, my little loaf.

Vague as fog and looked for like mail.
Farther off than Australia.
Bent-backed Atlas, our travelled prawn.
Snug as a bud and at home
Like a sprat in a pickle jug.
A creel of eels, all ripples.
Jumpy as a Mexican bean.
Right, like a well-done sum.
A clean slate, with your own face on.

*Sylvia Plath (1932–1963) was a leading American poet. Married to fellow poet Ted Hughes, Plath committed suicide at the age of 31, after several unsuccessful attempts. Her poetry and life has been the subject of many studies and films.*

POEM

# from Three Women

SYLVIA PLATH

... What did my fingers do before they held him?
What did my heart do, with its love?
I have never seen a thing so clear.
His lids are like the lilac-flower
And soft as a moth, his breath.
I shall not let go.
There is no guile or warp in him. May he keep so.

... I shall meditate upon normality.
I shall meditate upon my little son.
He does not walk. He does not speak a word.
He is still swaddled in white bands.
But he is pink and perfect. He smiles so frequently.
I have papered his room with big roses,
I have painted little hearts on everything.

I do not will him to be exceptional.
It is the exception that interests the devil.
It is the exception that climbs the sorrowful hill
Or sits in the desert and hurts his mother's heart.
I will him to be common,
To love me as I love him,
And to marry what he wants and where he will.

*This poem is set in a maternity ward and involves three women and
all three stanzas are from the first voice.*

# A Letter to Lady Margaret Cavendish Holles-Harley, When a Child

MATTHEW PRIOR

My noble, lovely, little Peggy,
Let this be my First Epistle beg ye,
At dawn of morn, and close of even,
To lift your heart and hands to Heaven.
In double beauty say your prayer:
*Our Father* first, then *Notre Père*.
And, dearest child, along the day,
In every thing you do and say,
Obey and please my lord and lady,
So God shall love and angels aid ye.

If to these precepts you attend,
No second letter need I send,
And so I rest your constant friend.

*Matthew Prior (1664–1721) was born in Dorset, England and worked for some time as a diplomat in The Hague. He is best remembered for his witty, light verse, although he also wrote other longer, more serious, poems.*

BIBLICAL

# Eat Honey

PROVERBS 24:13–14

13  Eat honey, my son, for it is good;
      honey from the comb is sweet to your taste.
14  Know also that wisdom is sweet to your soul;
      if you find it, there is future hope for you,
      and your hope will not be cut off.

BIBLICAL

# A Miktam of David

PSALM 16:5–8, 11

5   LORD, you have assigned me my portion and
     my cup; you have made my lot secure.
6   The boundary lines have fallen for me in pleasant
     places; surely I have a delightful inheritance.
7   I will praise the LORD, who counsels me;
     even at night my heart instructs me.
8   I have set the LORD always before me.
     Because he at my right hand,
     I will not be shaken.
11  You have made known to me the path of life;
     you will fill me with joy in your presence,
     with eternal pleasures at your right hand.

*New International Version*

## Of David

BIBLICAL

PSALM 37:3-6

3  Trust in the LORD and do good;
   dwell in the land and enjoy safe pasture.
4  Delight yourself in the LORD
    and he will give you the desires of your heart.
5  Commit your way to the LORD;
   trust in him and he will do this:
6  He will make your righteousness shine like the dawn,
    the justice of your cause like the noonday sun.

137

## Of Solomon

BIBLICAL

PSALM 127:3-5A

3  Sons are a heritage from the LORD,
   children are a reward from him.
4  Like arrows in the hands of a warrior
   are the sons born in one's youth.

5a Blessed is the man
   whose quiver is full of them.

*New International Version*

# Of David

PSALM 139:1—16

1  O LORD, you have searched me
    and you know me.

2  You know when I sit and when I rise;
    you perceive my thoughts from afar.

3  You discern my going out and my lying down
    you are familiar with all my ways.

4  Before a word is on my tongue
    you know it completely, O LORD.

5  You hem me in – behind and before;
    you have laid your hand upon me.

6  Such knowledge is too wonderful for me,
    too lofty for me to attain.

7  Where can I go from your Spirit?
    Where can I flee from your presence?

8  If I go up to the heavens, you are there;
    if I make my bed in the depths, you are there.

9  If I rise on the wings of the dawn,
    if I settle on the far side of the sea,

10  even there your hand will guide me,
    your right hand will hold me fast.

11  If I say, 'Surely the darkness will hide me
    and the light become night around me,'

12  even the darkness will not be dark to you;
    the night will shine like the day,
    for darkness is as light to you.

13 For you created my inmost being;
    you knit me together in my mother's womb.
14 I praise you because I am fearfully and
    wonderfully made; your works are wonderful,
    I know that full well.
15 My frame was not hidden from you
    when I was made in the secret place.
    When I was woven together in the depths
    of the earth,
16 your eyes saw my unformed body.
    All the days ordained for me
    were written in your book
    before one of them came to be.

139

*New International Version*

POEM

# Love Me, I Love You
## from Sing Song
CHRISTINA ROSSETTI

Love me, – I love you,
Love me, my baby;
Sing it high, sing it low,
Sing it as may be.

Mother's arms under you,
Her eyes above you;
Sing it high, sing it low,
Love me – I love you.

POEM

# I Know a Baby
## from Sing Song
CHRISTINA ROSSETTI

I know a baby, such a baby, –
Round blue eyes and cheeks of pink,
Such an elbow furrowed with dimples,
Such a wrist where creases sink.

'Cuddle and love me, cuddle and love me,'
Crows the mouth of coral pink:
Oh, the bald head, and, oh, the sweet lips,
And, oh, the sleepy eyes that wink!

*Christina Rossetti (1830–1894) came from a highly talented family and is viewed as one of the most important female poets of 19th-century England. These poems are taken from her collection of nursery rhymes,* Sing Song, *which was published in 1893.*

# from The Little Prince

ANTOINE DE SAINT-EXUPÉRY

... The little prince said, 'People start out in express trains, but they no longer know what they're looking for. Then they get all excited and rush around in circles ...' And he added, 'It's not worth the trouble ...'

The well we had come to was not at all like the wells of the Sahara. The wells of the Sahara are no more than holes dug in the sand. This one looked more like a village well. But there was no village here, and I thought I was dreaming.

'It's strange,' I said to the little prince, 'everything is ready: the pulley, the bucket, and the rope ...'

He laughed, grasped the rope, and set the pulley working. And the pulley groaned the way an old weather vane groans when the wind has been asleep a long time.

'Hear that?' said the little prince. 'We've awakened this well and it's singing.'

I didn't want him to tire himself out. 'Let me do that,' I said to him. 'It's too heavy for you.'

Slowly I hoisted the bucket to the edge of the well. I set it down with great care. The song of the pulley continued in my ears, and I saw the sun glisten on the still-trembling water.

'I'm thirsty for that water,' said the little prince. 'Let me drink some ...'

And I understood what he'd been looking for!

I raised the bucket to his lips. He drank, eyes closed. It was as sweet as a feast. That water was more than merely a drink. It was born of our walk beneath the stars, of the song of the pulley, of the effort in my arms. It did the heart

141

good, like a present. When I was a little boy, the Christmas-tree lights, the music of midnight mass, the tenderness of people's smiles made up, in the same way, the whole radiance of the Christmas present I received.

'People where you live,' the little prince said, 'grow five thousand roses in one garden ... yet they don't find what they're looking for ...'

'They don't find it,' I answered.

'And yet what they're looking for could be found in a single rose, or a little water ...'

'Of course,' I answered.

And the little prince added, 'But eyes are blind. You have to look with the heart.'

*Antoine de Saint-Exupéry (1900–1944) drew upon his experiences as a pilot in the Sahara desert to write and illustrate* The Little Prince, *a story about travelling the universe in order to understand life. Shortly after completing it, Saint-Exupéry went missing in his aircraft.*

# from The Wisdom of the Sands*

ANTOINE DE SAINT-EXUPÉRY

... In a house which becomes a home, one hands down
and another takes up the heritage of mind and heart,
laughter and tears, musings and deeds.

Love, like a carefully loaded ship, crosses the gulf
between the generations.

Let us bring up our children. It is not the place of
some official to hand them their heritage.

If others impart to our children our knowledge and
ideals, they will lose all of us that is wordless and full
of wonder.

Let us build memories in our children, lest they drag
out joyless lives, lest they allow treasures to be lost
because they have not been given the keys.

We live, not by things, but by the meaning of things.
It is needful to transmit the passwords from generation
to generation.

*Published posthumously in 1948, *The Wisdom of the Sands*
is a volume of reflections on mankind and civilisation.

POEM

# Little Girl, Be Careful What You Say

CARL SANDBURG

Little girl, be careful what you say
when you make talk with words, words –
for words are made of syllables, child, are made of air –
and air is so thin – air is the breath of God –
air is finer than fire or mist,
finer than water or moonlight,
finer than spider-webs in the moon,
finer than water-flowers in the morning;
and words are strong, too,
stronger than rocks or steel
stronger than potatoes, corn, fish, cattle,
and soft, too, soft as little pigeon-eggs,
soft as the music of hummingbird wings.
So, little girl, when you speak greetings,
when you tell jokes, make wishes or prayers,
be careful, be careless, be careful,
be what you want to be.

**144**

*Carl Sandburg (1878–1967) was an American poet, novelist, historian and folklorist. He won two Pulitzer prizes in his lifetime.*

# A Child's Prayer

SIEGFRIED SASSOON

POEM

For Morn, my dome of blue,
For Meadows, green and gay,
And Birds who love the twilight of the leaves,
Let Jesus keep me joyful when I pray.

For the big Bees that hum
And hide in bells of flowers;
For the winding roads that come
To Evening's holy door,
May Jesus bring me grateful to his arms,
And guard my innocence for evermore.

145

*Siegfried Sassoon (1886–1967) was an English poet and writer. His experience of fighting in the First World War (1914–1918) greatly affected his outlook on life, and it was his anti-war poetry and public affirmation of pacifism that made him widely known.*

POEM

# Sonnet XV

WILLIAM SHAKESPEARE

When I consider everything that grows
Holds in perfection but a little moment,
That this huge stage presenteth naught but shows
Whereon the stars in secret influence comment;
When I perceive that men as plants increase,
Cheerèd and checked even by the selfsame sky;
Vaunt in their youthful sap, at height decrease,
And wear their brave state out of memory:
Then the conceit of this inconstant stay
Sets you most rich in youth before my sight,
Where wasteful time debateth with decay
To change your day of youth to sullied night;
And all in war with time for love of you,
As he takes from you. I engraft you anew.

*William Shakespeare* (1564–1616) *playwright and poet, has had his work studied more than that of any other author writing in the English language. He wrote this sonnet about the perfection of a young person and his defeat of the passage of time with this timeless verse that keeps his youthful beauty fresh.*

# To My Daughter

STEPHEN SPENDER

POEM

Bright clasp of her whole hand around my finger,
My daughter, as we walk together now.
All my life I'll feel a ring invisibly
Circle this bone with shining: when she is grown
Far from today as her eyes are far already.

*Stephen Spender (1909–1995) was a leading 20th-century English poet, writer and social commentator. His earliest success was in the 1930s – a decade in which he witnessed the Spanish civil war and the outbreak of the Second World War (1939–1945). Much of his work reflects the great interest he took in politics.*

SPIRITUAL

# Be Happy (1)

SRI CHINMOY

Be happy!
You will grow into God's greatest blessing,
His highest pride.
Be happy!

Yesterday's world wants you to enjoy its surrendering breath.
Today's world wants you to enjoy its surrendered breath.
Tomorrow's world wants you to enjoy its fulfilling breath.

Be happy!
Be happy in the morning with what you have.
Be happy in the evening with what you are.
Be happy!

Do not complain. Who complains? The blind beggar in you.
When you complain, you dance in the mire of ignorance.
When you do not complain, all conditions of the world are at
your feet,
and God gives you a new name: aspiration.
Aspiration is the supreme wealth in the world
of light and delight.

Be happy!
Do you want never to be poor? Then be happy.
Do you want ever to be great? Then be happy.
Be happy!

You will get what you like most.
You will get what you like best.
Be happy!

God sees in you His aspiring creation.
His transforming realisation,
His illumining revelation,
and His fulfilling manifestation.

Be happy!

Be happy!

God sees in you another God.
God sees you as another God.
God sees you and Him as one.

# Be Happy (2)
SRI CHINMOY

Be happy, be happy!
Unless you are happy,
Your outer life will not succeed
And your inner life will not proceed.

SPIRITUAL

*Sri Chinmoy (b. 1931) was born in Bangladesh and spent much of
his early life in a spiritual community in southern India before travelling
to New York in 1964. His poetry is concerned with spiritual consciousness
and expressing the inexpressible.*

POEM

# Étude Réaliste

ALGERNON CHARLES SWINBURNE

I

A baby's feet, like sea-shells pink,
Might tempt, should heaven see meet,
An angel's lips to kiss, we think,
A baby's feet.

Like rose-hued sea-flowers toward the heat
They stretch and spread and wink
Their ten soft buds that part and meet.

No flower-bells that expand and shrink
Gleam half so heavenly sweet
As shine on life's untrodden brink
A baby's feet.

II

A baby's hands, like rosebuds furled
Whence yet no leaf expands,
Ope if you touch, though close upcurled,
A baby's hands.

Then, fast as warriors grip their brands
When battle's bolt is hurled,
They close, clenched hard like tightening bands.

No rosebuds yet by dawn impearled
Match, even in loveliest lands,
The sweetest flowers in all the world –
A baby's hands.

III

A baby's eyes, ere speech begin,
Ere lips learn words or sighs,
Bless all things bright enough to win
A baby's eyes.

Love, while the sweet thing laughs and lies,
And sleep flows out and in,
Sees perfect in them Paradise.

Their glance might cast out pain and sin,
Their speech make dumb the wise,
By mute glad godhead felt within
A baby's eyes.

*Algernon Charles Swinburne (1837–1909) was a Victorian poet whose work is known for its rhythmic and melodious qualities and have often been said to have an almost narcotic affect. Swinburne was pagan in his sympathies.*

# The Beginning

RABINDRANATH TAGORE

'Where have I come from, where did you pick me up?'
the baby asked its mother.
She answered, half crying, half laughing, and clasping the
baby to her breast –
'You were hidden in my heart as its desire, my darling.
You were in the dolls of my childhood's games; and when
with clay I made the image of my god every morning, I made
the unmade you then.
You were enshrined with our household deity, in his worship
I worshipped you.
In all my hopes and my loves, in my life, in the life of my
mother you have lived.
In the lap of the deathless Spirit who rules our home you
have been nursed for ages.
When in girlhood my heart was opening its petals, you
hovered as a fragrance about it.
Your tender softness bloomed in my youthful limbs, like
a glow in the sky before the sunrise.
Heaven's first darling, twain-born with the morning light,
you have floated down the stream of the world's life, and
at last you have stranded on my heart.
As I gaze on your face, mystery overwhelms me; you who
belong to all have become mine.
For fear of losing you I hold you tight to my breast.
What magic has snared the world's treasure in these slender
arms of mine?'

*Rabindranath Tagore (1861–1941) was an Indian poet and philosopher. He founded a communal school where he aimed to blend eastern and western philosophical and educational systems, and he received the Nobel Prize for literature in 1913.*

# The Child-Angel

RABINDRANATH TAGORE

They clamour and fight, they doubt and despair,
they know no end to their wrangling.
Let your life come amongst them like a flame of light,
my child, unflickering and pure, and delight them
into silence.
They are cruel in their greed and their envy, their
words are like hidden knives thirsting for blood.
Go and stand amidst their scowling hearts, my child,
and let your gentle eyes fall upon them like the forgiving
peace of the evening over the strife of the day.
Let them see your face, my child, and thus know the
meaning of all things; let them love you and thus love
each other.
Come and take your seat in the bosom of the limitless,
my child. At sunrise open and raise your heart like a
blossoming flower, and at sunset bend your head and
in silence complete the worship of the day.

SPIRITUAL

# The Gift

RABINDRANATH TAGORE

I want to give you something, my child, for we are drifting
in the stream of the world.
Our lives will be carried apart, and our love forgotten.
But I am not so foolish as to hope that I could buy your
heart with my gifts.
Young is your life, your path long, and you drink the love
we bring you at one draught and turn and run away from us.
You have your play and your playmates. What harm is there
if you have no time or thought for us!
We, indeed, have leisure enough in old age to count the
days that are past, to cherish in our hearts what our hands
have lost for ever.
The river runs swift with a song, breaking through all
barriers. But the mountain stays and remembers, and
follows her with his love.

# Spirit of Affirmation

POEM

CECILY TAYLOR

I am the way that stretches out before –
I am the journey you are on,
I am the present moment that you tread –
I am the next place that you stand upon.

I am the air you breathe –
I am every part and of the whole,
I am the love you cannot fall beyond –
I am the inner silence of your soul.

I am the question that you ask –
I am the answer that you crave,
I am the reality of truth,
I am the ever-living thread that leaps the grave.

I am all time in now,
I am this minute to begin,
I am the one that you have always known;
I am the peace that you may dwell within.

*Cecily Taylor (b. 1930) has been involved in Early Years Education, community relations and minority rights, and her songs for worship and poems have been published widely. This blessing is based on an Irish Mother's Blessing.*

SPIRITUAL

# Kiss the Earth

THICH NHAT HANH

Walk and touch peace every moment.
Walk and touch happiness every moment.
Each step brings a fresh breeze.
Each step makes a flower bloom.
Kiss the Earth with your feet.
Bring the Earth your love and happiness.
The Earth will be safe
when we feel safe in ourselves.

*Thich Nhat Hanh (b. 1926) is a Vietnamese Buddhist monk and a peace activist who lives in France. He was nominated by Martin Luther King, Jr. for the Nobel Peace prize in 1967.*

# from His Nobel Lecture, 1984

ARCHBISHOP DESMOND TUTU

PRAYER

... God created us for fellowship. God created us so
that we should form the human family, existing
together because we were made for one another.
We are not made for an exclusive self-sufficiency
but for interdependence, and we break the law of
our being at our peril.

God calls us to be fellow workers with Him, so
that we can extend His Kingdom of Shalom, of
justice, of goodness, of compassion, of caring,
of sharing, of laughter, joy and reconciliation,
so that the kingdoms of this world will become
the Kingdom of our God and of His Christ, and
He shall reign forever and ever.

Amen.

157

*Archbishop Desmond Tutu (b. 1931) was born in South Africa
and became the first black South African Anglican Archbishop of Cape
Town in 1986. He gave this lecture on December 11, 1984, after winning
the Nobel Peace Prize earlier that year.*

# from the Declaration of the Rights of the Child

UNITED NATIONS

... We owe to children the best we have to give.

You are entitled, without exception, to these rights, whatever your race, colour, sex, language, religion, political or other opinion, nationality, property, wherever you were born and whoever your family is:

You need special protection, and to be given the opportunity to develop physically, mentally, morally, spiritually and socially in a healthy and normal manner in a free and dignified way. Your best interests should be of paramount consideration.

You are entitled from birth to a name and a nationality.

You are entitled to good health, security, adequate nutrition, housing, recreation and medical services.

You have the right to special care if you are handicapped in any way.

You need love and understanding for your character to develop properly. You should grow up in the care of your family in an atmosphere of affection and moral and material security, and if you don't have a family the state has a duty to care for you.

You are entitled to an education, which should be free and give you a chance to be able to develop your abilities, judgment, and sense of moral and social responsibility so that you can become a valued member of society.

Your best interests must be the guiding principle of your parents and those responsible for your education and guidance. You have the right to be able to play and enjoy activities, and always to be protected and helped.

You need to be protected against all forms of neglect, cruelty and exploitation, child labour or anything else that could jeopardize your health or education, or interfere with your physical, mental or moral development.

You need to be protected from racial, religious and any other discriminatory practices. You should be brought up in a spirit of understanding, tolerance, friendship, peace and universal brotherhood, with an awareness that your energy and talents can help make a difference to others.

The Declaration of the Rights of the Child *was adopted unanimously on 20 November 1959 by the General Assembly of the United Nations.*

POEM

# Four Things

HENRY VAN DYKE

Four things a man must learn to do
If he would make his record true:
To think without confusion clearly;
To love his fellow man sincerely;
To act from honest motives purely;
To trust in God and Heaven securely.

*Henry Van Dyke (1852–1933) was an American poet and writer.*
*He initially trained and worked as a Presbyterian minister, and later became*
*a university lecturer. His faith is evident as a theme in this poem and in much*
*of his other work.*

# Before You Knew You Owned It

POEM

ALICE WALKER

Expect nothing. Live frugally
On surprise.
become a stranger
To need of pity
Or, if compassion be freely
Given out
Take only enough
Stop short of urge to plead
Then purge away the need.

Wish for nothing larger
Than your own small heart
Or greater than a star;
Tame wild disappointment
With caress unmoved and cold
Make of it a parka
For your soul.

Discover the reason why
So tiny human midget
Exists at all
So scared unwise
But expect nothing. Live frugally
On surprise.

*Alice Walker (b. 1944) is an African American Pulitzer prize-winning author and poet. She defines herself as, amongst other things, a womanist – a term that she created to define the experiences of women of colour. She is probably most famous for her novel,* The Colour Purple.

HYMN

# from A Cradle Hymn

ISAAC WATTS

Hush! My dear, lie still and slumber,
Holy angels guard thy bed!
Heavenly blessings without number
Gently falling on thy head.

Sleep, my babe; thy food and raiment,
House and home, thy friends provide;
All without thy care or payment:
All thy wants are well supplied.

*Isaac Watts (1674–1748) was a poet and a preacher. He wrote around 700 hymns, including 'When I Survey the Wondrous Cross' and 'Our God, Our Help in Ages Past'.*

# from There Was a Child Went Forth

POEM

WALT WHITMAN

... There was a child went forth every day;
And the first object he look'd upon, that object he became,
And that object became part of him for the day, or a certain
    part of the day,
Or for many years, or stretching cycles of years.

The early lilacs became part of this child,
And grass and white and red morning-glories, and white
    and red clover, and the song of the phoebe-bird,
And the March-born lambs and the sow's pink-faint litter,
    and the mare's foal, and the cow's calf,
And the noisy brood of the barnyard or by the mire of
    the pondside,
And the fish suspending themselves so curiously below
    there, and the beautiful curious liquid,
And the water-plants with their graceful flat heads, all
    became part of him.

The field-sprouts of April and May became part of him,
Winter-grain sprouts and those of the light-yellow corn,
    and the esculent roots of the garden,
And the appletrees cover'd with blossoms and the fruit
    afterward, and woodberries, and the commonest weeds
    by the road ...

The family usages, the language, the company, the furniture,
    the yearning and swelling heart,

Affection that will not be gainsay'd, the sense of what is real,
the thought if after all it should prove unreal,
The doubts of daytime and the doubts of night-time, the
curious whether and how,
Whether that which appears so is so, or is it all flashes
and specks?
Men and women crowding fast in the streets, if they are not
flashes and specks what are they?
The streets themselves and the façades of houses, and goods
in the windows,
Vehicles, teams, the heavy-plank'd wharves, the huge crossing
at the ferries,
The village on the highland seen from afar at sunset, the
river between,
Shadows, aureola and mist, the light falling on roofs and
gables of white or brown two miles off,
The schooner near by sleepily dropping down the tide, the
little boat slack-towed astern,
The hurrying tumbling waves, quick-broken crests, slapping,
The strata of colour'd clouds, the long bar of maroon-tint,
away solitary by itself, the spread of purity it lies motionless in,
The horizon's edge, the flying sea-crow, the fragrance of salt
marsh and shore mud,
These became part of that child who went forth every day,
and who now goes, and will always go forth every day.

*Walt Whitman (1819–1892) was a groundbreaking American poet.
He abandoned rhyme and metre using free verse in opposition to the
structured European poetic styles of the time. His poetry speaks on issues
such as democracy, war, politics, race and slavery.*

# Progress

ELLA WHEELER WILCOX

Let there be many windows to your soul,
That all the glory of the universe
May beautify it. Not the narrow pane
Of one poor creed can catch the radiant rays
That shine from countless sources. Tear away
The blinds of superstition; let the light
Pour through fair windows broad as truth itself
And high as God.

Why should the spirit peer
Through some priest-curtained orifice, and grope
Along dim corridors of doubt, when all
The splendour from unfathomed seas of space
Might bathe it with the golden waves of Love?
Sweep up the debris of decaying faiths;
Sweep down the cobwebs of worn-out beliefs,
And throw your soul wide open to the light
Of Reason and of knowledge. Tune your ear
To all the wordless music of the stars,
And to the voice of Nature; and your heart
Shall turn to truth and goodness as the plant
Turns to the sun. A thousand unseen hands
Reach down to help you to their peace-crowned heights,
And all the forces of the firmament
Shall fortify your strength. Be not afraid
To thrust aside half-truths and grasp the whole.

*Ella Wheeler Wilcox (1850–1919) was a popular American poet and journalist in her lifetime. Her first published work, some sketches in the* New York Mercury, *appeared when she was 14 years old. Her clearly written, rhyming poems often convey a sense of optimism and hope.*

# Show Me the Way

ELLA WHEELER WILCOX

Show me the way that leads to the true life,
I do not care what tempests may assail me,
I shall be given courage for the strife,
I know my strength will not desert or fail me;
I know that I shall conquer in the fray:
                              Show me the way.

Show me the way up to a higher plane,
Where body shall be servant to the soul.
I do not care what tides of woe, or pain,
Across my life their angry waves may roll
If I but reach the end I seek some day:
                              Show me the way.

Show me the way, and let me bravely climb
Above vain grievings for unworthy treasures;
Above all sorrow that finds balm in time –
Above small triumphs, or belittling pleasures;
Up to those heights where these things seem child's play:
                              Show me the way.

Show me the way to that calm, perfect peace
Which springs form an inward consciousness of right;
To where all conflicts with the flesh shall cease,
And self shall radiate with the spirit's light.
Though hard the journey and the strife, I pray
                              Show me the way.

# Wishes for a Little Girl

POEM

ELLA WHEELER WILCOX

What would I ask the kindly fates to give
To crown her life, if I could have my way?
My strongest wishes would be negative,
If they would but obey.

Give her not greatness. For great souls must stand
Alone and lonely in this little world;
Cleft rocks that show the great Creator's hand,
Thither by earthquakes hurled.

Give her not genius. Spare her the cruel pain
Of finding her whole life a prey for daws;
Of bearing with quickened sense and burning brain
The world's sneer-tinged applause.

Give her not perfect beauty's gifts. For then
Her truthful mirror would infuse her mind
With love for self, and for the praise of men,
That lowers woman-kind.

But make her fair and comely to the sight,
Give her more heart than brain, more love than pride,
Let her be tender-thoughted, cheerful, bright,
Some strong ma's star and guide.

Not vainly questioning why she was sent
Into this restless world of toil and strife,
Let her go bravely on her way, content
To make the best of life.

Song

# Isn't She Lovely

## STEVIE WONDER

Isn't she lovely
Isn't she wonderful
Isn't she precious
Less than one minute old
I never thought through love we'd be
Making one as lovely as she
But isn't she lovely made from love

Isn't she pretty
Truly the angel's best
Boy, I'm so happy
We have been heaven blessed
I can't believe what God has done
Through us he's given life to one
But isn't she lovely made from love

Isn't she lovely
Life and love are the same
Life is Aisha
The meaning of her name
Londie, it could have not been done
Without you who conceived the one
That's so very lovely made from love

*Stevie Wonder (b. 1950) is an American singer, songwriter, multi-instrumentalist and one of the most creative musical figures today. This song was written for his daughter Aisha and appears in the album* Songs in the Key of Life.

# Composed on a May Morning, 1838

WILLIAM WORDSWORTH

LIFE with you Lambs, like day, is just begun,
Yet Nature seems to them a heavenly guide.
Does joy approach? they meet the coming tide;
And sullenness avoid, as now they shun
Pale twilight's lingering glooms -- and in the sun
Couch near their dams, with quiet satisfied;
Or gambol -- each with his shadow at his side,
Varying its shape wherever he may run.
As they from turf yet hoar with sleepy dew
All turn, and court the shining and the green,
Where herbs look up, and opening flowers are seen;
Why to God's goodness cannot We be true,
And so, His gifts and promises between,
Feed to the last on pleasures ever new?

*William Wordsworth (1770–1850) was credited with ushering in the English Romantic Movement with the publication of* Lyrical Ballads *(1798) in collaboration with Samuel Taylor Coleridge (see pages 59–62). Together with Coleridge, Wordsworth wrote poetry that explored the divine aspects of nature.*

POEM

# from Ode: Intimations of Immortality from Recollections of Early Childhood

WILLIAM WORDSWORTH

V

Our birth is but a sleep and a forgetting;
The Soul that rises with us, our life's Star,
    Hath had elsewhere its setting
      And cometh from afar:
    Not in entire forgetfulness,
    And not in utter nakedness,
But trailing clouds of glory do we come
    From God, who is our home:
Heaven lies about us in our infancy!
Shades of the prison-house begin to close
    Upon the growing Boy,
But he beholds the light, and whence it flows,
    He sees it in his joy;
The Youth, who daily farther from the east
    Must travel, still is Nature's priest,
    And by the vision splendid
    Is on his way attended;
At length the Man perceives it die away,
And fade into the light of common day.

VI

Earth fills her lap with pleasures of her own;
Yearnings she hath in her own natural kind,

And, even with something of a Mother's mind,
    And no unworthy aim,
    The homely Nurse doth all she can
To make her Foster-child, her Inmate Man,
    Forget the glories he hath known,
And that imperial palace whence he came.

VII

Behold the Child among his new-born blisses,
A six years' Darling of a pigmy size!
See, where 'mid work of his own hand he lies,
Fretted by sallies of his mother's kisses,
With light upon him from his father's eyes!
See, at his feet, some little plan or chart,
Some fragment from his dream of human life,
Shaped by himself with newly-learnéd art;
    A wedding or a festival,
    A mourning or a funeral;
      And this hath now his heart,
    And unto this he frames his song:
      Then will he fit his tongue
To dialogues of business, love, or strife;
    But it will not be long

Ere this be thrown aside,
　　And with new joy and pride
The little Actor cons another part;
Filling from time to time his 'humorous stage'
With all the Persons, down to palsied Age,
That Life brings with her in her equipage;
　　As if his whole vocation
　　Were endless imitation ...

XI
And O, ye Fountains, Meadows, Hills, and Groves,
Forebode not any severing of our loves!
Yet in my heart of hearts I feel your might;
I only have relinquished one delight
To live beneath your more habitual sway;
I love the Brooks which down their channels fret,
Even more than when I tripped lightly as they;
The innocent brightness of a new-born Day
　　Is lovely yet;
The Clouds that gather round the setting sun
Do take a sober colouring from an eye
That hath kept watch o'er man's mortality;
Another race hath been, and other palms are won.
Thanks to the human heart by which we live,
Thanks to its tenderness, its joys, and fears,
To me the meanest flower that blows can give
Thoughts that do often lie too deep for tears.

# The Character of a Happy Life

POEM

SIR HENRY WOTTON

How happy is he born and taught
That serveth not another's will;
Whose armour is his honest thought,
And simple truth his utmost skill!

Whose passions not his masters are;
Whose soul is still prepared for death,
Untied unto the world by care
Of public fame or private breath;

Who envies none that chance doth raise,
Nor vice; who never understood
How deepest wounds are given by praise;
Nor rules of state, but rules of good;

Who hath his life from rumours freed;
Whose conscience in his strong retreat;
Whose state can neither flatterers feed,
Nor ruin make oppressors great;

Who God doth late and early pray
More of His grace than gifts to lend;
And entertains the harmless day
With a religious book or friend;

– This man is freed from servile bands
Of hope to rise or fear to fall:
Lord of himself, though not of lands,
And having nothing, yet hath all.

174

_Sir Henry Wotton (1568–1639) was an English poet, diplomat, and art connoisseur who was a friend of the English poets John Donne and John Milton._

# Woman to Child

JUDITH WRIGHT

POEM

You who were darkness warmed my flesh
where out of darkness rose the seed.
Then all a world I made in me;
all the world you hear and see
hung upon my dreaming blood.

There moved the multitudinous stars,
and coloured birds and fishes moved.
There swam the sliding continents.
All time lay rolled in me, and sense,
and love that knew not its beloved.

O node and focus of the world;
I hold you deep within that well
you shall escape and not escape –
that mirrors still your sleeping shape;
that nurtures still your crescent cell.

I wither and you break from me;
yet though you dance in living light
I am the earth, I am the root,
I am the stem that fed the fruit,
the link that joins you to the night.

*Judith Wright (1915–2000) was a major Australian poet who revealed a great love of the environment, and the relationship between the land and mankind, through her poetry. After the birth of her daughter, she also wrote a series of books for children.*

POEM

# A Cradle Song
W.B. YEATS

The angels are stooping
Above your bed;
They weary of trooping
With the whimpering dead.
God's laughing in Heaven
To see you so good;
The Sailing Sven
Are gay with His mood.
I sigh that kiss you,
For I must own
That I shall miss you
When you have grown.

*W.B. Yeats (1865–1939) was one of the founders of the Irish Literary Revival. His poetry draws upon Irish myth and legend and a glorified image of the peasant. He received the Nobel Prize for Literature in 1923.*

# from A Prayer for My Daughter

POEM

W.B. YEATS

Once more the storm is howling, and half hid
Under this cradle-hood and coverlid
My child sleeps on. There is no obstacle
But Gregory's wood and one bare hill
Whereby the haystack- and roof-levelling wind,
Bred on the Atlantic, can be stayed;
And for an hour I have walked and prayed
Because of the great gloom that is in my mind.

I have walked and prayed for this young child an hour
And heard the sea-wind scream upon the tower,
And – under the arches of the bridge, and scream
In the elms above the flooded stream;
Imagining in excited reverie
That the future years had come,
Dancing to a frenzied drum,
Out of the murderous innocence of the sea.

May she be granted beauty and yet not
Beauty to make a stranger's eye distraught,
Or hers before a looking-glass, for such,
Being made beautiful overmuch,
Consider beauty a sufficient end,
Lose natural kindness and maybe
The heart-revealing intimacy
That chooses right, and never find a friend ...

In courtesy I'd have her chiefly learned;
Hearts are not had as a gift but hearts are earned
By those that are not entirely beautiful;
Yet many, that have played the fool
For beauty's very self, has charm made wise.
And many a poor man that has roved,
Loved and thought himself beloved,
From a glad kindness cannot take his eyes.

May she become a flourishing hidden tree
That all her thoughts may like the linnet be,
And have no business but dispensing round
Their magnanimities of sound,
Nor but in merriment begin a chase,
Nor but in merriment a quarrel.
O may she live like some green laurel
Rooted in one dear perpetual place ...

An intellectual hatred is the worst,
So let her think opinions are accursed.
Have I not seen the loveliest woman born
Out of the mouth of plenty's horn,
Because of her opinionated mind
Barter that horn and every good
By quiet natures understood
For an old bellows full of angry wind?

Considering that, all hatred driven hence,
The soul recovers radical innocence
And learns at last that it is self-delighting,
Self-appeasing, self-affrighting,
And that its own sweet will is Heaven's will;
She can, though every face should scowl
And every windy quarter howl
Or every bellows burst, be happy Still.

And may her bridegroom bring her to a house
Where all's accustomed, ceremonious;
For arrogance and hatred are the wares
Peddled in the thoroughfares.
How but in custom and in ceremony
Are innocence and beauty born?
Ceremony's a name for the rich horn,
And custom for the spreading laurel tree.

# Quotations on Children, Wisdom and Names

## ON CHILDREN

*'It takes a village to raise a child.'*
– African proverb

*'Never lend your car to anyone to whom
you have given birth.'*
– Erma Bombeck (1927–1996), writer

*'A mother's love for her child is like nothing else in
the world. It knows no law, no pity, it dares
all things and crushes down remorselessly
all that stands in its path.'*
– Agatha Christie (1890–1976), writer

*'Parents can only give good advice or put them on
the right paths, but the final forming of a person's
character lies in their own hands.'*
– Anne Frank (1929–1945), diarist

*'When you are a mother, you are never really alone
in your thoughts. A mother always has to think
twice, once for herself and once for her child.'*
– Sophia Loren (b. 1934), actor

*'There can be no keener revelation of a society's soul
than the way in which it treats its children.'*
– Nelson Mandela (b. 1918),
lawyer and statesman

*'The childhood shows the man, as
morning shows the day.'*
– John Milton, (1608–1674), poet

*'You know your children are growing up when they
stop asking you where they came from and refuse
to tell you where they are going.'*
– P.J. O'Rourke (b.1947), satirist

*'A child educated only at school is an uneducated child.'*
– George Santayana (1863–1952), philosopher,
poet and novelist

*'Making the decision to have a child – it's momentous.
It is to decide forever to have your heart
go walking outside your body.'*
– Elizabeth Stone, author and teacher

*'We are always too busy for our children; we never
give them the time or interest they deserve. We lavish
gifts upon them; but the most precious gift –
our personal association, which means so
much to them – we give grudgingly.'*
– Mark Twain (1835–1910), writer

## ON WISDOM AND
## ADVICE ON LIFE

*'Far away there in the sunshine are my highest aspirations.
I may not reach them, but I can look up
and see their beauty, believe in them, and
try to follow where they lead.'*
– Louisa May Alcott (1832–1888), writer

*'Success is never final. Failure is never fatal.
It is courage that counts.'*
– Winston Churchill (1874–1965),
statesman

*'It doesn't matter how slowly you go up,
so long as you do not stop.'*
– Confucius (551–479 BC), philosopher

*'All our dreams can come true – if we have
the courage to pursue them.'*
– Walt Disney (1901–1966), artist
and film producer

*'If we did the things we are capable of, we
would astound ourselves.'*
– Thomas Edison (1847–1931),
inventor and physicist

*'There are only two ways to live your life. One is as
though nothing is a miracle. The other is as though
everything is a miracle.'*
– Albert Einstein (1879–1955),
mathematical physicist

*'It's not what happens to you, but how
you react to it that matters.'*
– Epictetus (1st century AD), philosopher

*'Be careful to leave your sons well instructed rather
than rich, for the hopes of the instructed are better
than the wealth of the ignorant.'*
– Epictetus

*'Happiness is when what you think, what you say
and what you do are in harmony.'*
– Mahatma Gandhi (1869–1948), leader

*'Whatever you can do, or dream you can, begin it.
Boldness has genius, power and magic in it.'*
– Johann Wolfgang von Goethe (1749–1832),
poet, dramatist and scientist

*'I expect to pass through this world but once. Any good
things, therefore, that I can do, any kindness I can
show to a fellow being, let me do it now. Let me not
defer or neglect it for I shall not pass this way again.'*
– Stephen Grellet (1773–1855), Quaker
and missionary

*'What lies behind us and what lies before us are tiny matters
compared to what lies within us.'*
– Oliver Wendell Holmes (1809–1894),
physician and writer

*'A moment's insight is sometimes worth a life's experience.'*
– Oliver Wendell Holmes

*'Act as if what you do makes a difference. It does.'*
– William James (1842–1910), philosopher

*'A good head and a good heart are always a
formidable combination.'*
– Nelson Mandela

*'Life shrinks or expands in proportion to one's courage.'*
– Anaïs Nin (1903–1977), writer

'The only journey is the one within.'
– Rainer Maria Rilke (1875–1926), poet

'The future belongs to those who believe in the
beauty of their dreams.'
– Eleanor Roosevelt (1884–1962), humanitarian
and wife of US President Franklin D. Roosevelt

'No one can make you feel inferior without your consent.'
– Eleanor Roosevelt

'Lead the life that will make you kindly and friendly
to everyone about you, and you will be surprised
what a happy life you will lead.'
– Charles M. Schwab (1862–1939), businessman

'Be who you are and say what you feel, because those
who mind don't matter and those who matter don't mind.'
– Dr Seuss (1904–1991), children's
author and illustrator

'Let no one ever come to you without leaving better
and happier. Be the living expression of God's
kindness: kindness in your face, kindness in
your eyes, kindness in your smile.'
– Mother Teresa (1910–1997) Roman Catholic
nun and missionary

'I teach my child to look at life in a thoroughly materialistic
fashion. If he escapes and becomes the sort of person I
hope he will become, it will be because he sees
through the hokum that I hand out.'
– Elwyn Brooks White (1899–1985), essayist,
novelist and poet

*'The secret of contentment is knowing how to enjoy
what you have, and to be able to lose all desire
for things beyond your reach.'*
– Lin Yutang (1895–1967), writer
and inventor

*'Quit now, you'll never make it. If you disregard this
advice, you'll be halfway there.'*
– David Zucker (b. 1947), director

## ON NAMES

*'Action without a name, a who attached to it,
is meaningless.'*
– Hannah Arendt (1906–1975),
philosopher

*'A good name is better than fine perfume.'*
– Ecclesiastes 7.1

*'I never liked the name Eldred. Since nobody knew me in
New York, I just changed to my middle name.'*
≠– Gregory Peck (1916–2003), actor

*'What's in a name? That which we call a rose
By any other name would smell as sweet.'*
– William Shakespeare (1564–1616), playwright,
poet and actor

*'I don't want to lose my name because that's how I
know myself. There is a legacy here.'*
Moon Unit Zappa (b. 1967), actor, author
and musician

# Acknowledgements

I'd like to thank Rev. Malcolm Newman, Rev. Mark Hargreaves and Rev. Christine Robinson for their help and advice, Julia Shone and Aruna Vasudevan at New Holland Publishers, and James for his great suggestions and endless support.

'You Begin' by Margaret Atwood; In the US: from *Selected Poems II: Poems Selected and New, 1976-1986* by Margaret Atwood. Copyright © 1987 by Margaret Atwood. Reprinted by permission of Houghton Mifflin Company. All rights reserved. In the British Commonwealth reproduced with permission of Curtis Brown Group Ltd, London. In Canada reproduced with permission of Oxford University Press Canada. All rights reserved. 'A Newborn Child at Passover' from *Rope Bridge* by Nan Cohen © 2005 Cherry Grove Collections, Cincinnati, Ohio, USA. 'Ode on the Whole Duty of Parents' from *Selected Poems* by Frances Cornford. Reprinted by permission of Enitharmon Press, 1996). 'may my heart always be open to little' is reprinted from *Complete Poems 1904–1962*, By E.E. Cummings, edited by George J. Firmage, by permission of W.W. Norton and Company, Copyright © 1991 by the Trustees for the E.E. Cummings Trust and George James. 'Learning to Talk' from *The Complete Poems* by C. Day Lewis, published by Sinclair-Stevenson (1992) Copyright © 1992 in this edition The Estate of C. Day Lewis. Reprinted by permission of The Random House Group Ltd. 'That Love Is All There Is' and 'In This Short Life' by Emily Dickinson, reprinted by permission of the publishers and the Trustees of Amherst College from *The Poems Of Emily Dickinson*, Thomas H. Johnson, ed., Cambridge, Mass.: The Belknap Press of Harvard University Press,

Sassoon by kind permission of the Estate of George Sassoon. 'To My Daughter' from *New Collected Poems* by Stephen Spender © 2004. Reprinted with the kind permission of the Estate of Stephen Spender. 'The Beginning', 'The Child-Angel' and 'The Gift' by Rabindranath Tagore, reprinted by permission of the Sahitya Akademi. 'Spirit of Affirmation' by Cecily Taylor. Copyright © Cecily Taylor. Reprinted by kind permission of Cecily Taylor. 'A Cradle Song' and extract from 'A Prayer For My Daughter' by W.B. Yeats reproduced by permission of A.P. Watt Ltd on behalf of Grainne Yeats. Scripture quotations taken from the Holy Bible, *New International Version*. Copyright © 1973, 1978, 1984 by International Bible Society. Used by permission of Hodder & Stoughton Publishers, A member of the Hachette Livre UK Group. All rights reserved.

# Index of First Lines